Patterns of Change in Developing Rural Regions

About the Book and Editors

Development specialists often overlook the fact that the towns of a rural region play as essential a role in the region's economy as does agriculture, and they design and implement broad strategies without due recognition of the unique and dynamic character of each individual region. Proper analysis requires consideration of the changing nature of rural regions and the principal agents of change. The contributors to this volume argue that development strategists should focus on processes rather than on products by taking the nonfarm aspects, as well as the farm aspects, of rural development into account and by recognizing that land, labor, water, and technology do not alone lead to balanced regional and agricultural development. The analytical approaches presented in this book incorporate wide-ranging variables from the urban space of rural regions—markets, towns, service industries, and organizations—that have major impacts on the rural regional economy. These methodologies aim at improving rural regional development processes.

Raphael Bar-El is an economist at the Settlement Study Centre and a professor at Ben-Gurion University. **Avrom Bendavid-Val** is an international consultant in the field of regional development planning; he is currently on assignment as an economist with the Settlement and Resource Systems Analysis Project at Clark University. **Gerald J. Karaska** is professor of geography and director of the Settlement and Resource Systems Analysis Project at Clark University.

Published in cooperation with
the Settlement Study Centre (SSC)

Patterns of Change in Developing Rural Regions

edited by Raphael Bar-El,
Avrom Bendavid-Val,
and Gerald J. Karaska

Routledge
Taylor & Francis Group
LONDON AND NEW YORK

First published 1987 by Westview Press

Published 2019 by Routledge
52 Vanderbilt Avenue, New York, NY 10017
2 Park Square, Milton Park, Abingdon, Oxon OX14 4RN

Routledge is an imprint of the Taylor & Francis Group, an informa business

Library of Congress Cataloging-in-Publication Data
Patterns of change in developing rural regions.
(Westview special studies in social, political, and economic development)
1. Rural development—Developing countries. 2. Developing countries—Economic conditions. 3. Regional planning—Developing countries. 4. Regional economics. I. Bar-El, Raphael. II. Bendavid-Val, Avrom. III. Karaska, Gerald J. IV. Series.
HN981.C6P38 1987 307.7′2′091724 86-18986

ISBN 13: 978-0-367-28243-1 (hbk)
ISBN 13: 978-0-367-29789-3 (pbk)

TABLE OF CONTENTS

INTRODUCTION

In 1981, Clark University at Worcester, Massachussets, and the Institute for Development Anthropology at Binghamton, New York, entered into a 'Cooperative Agreement' with the US Agency for International Development (USAID) to study regional development, provide technical assistance to Third World countries through USAID programs and field Missions, mount training programs and hold scholarly symposia on regional development. This agreement bears the title 'Settlement and Resource Systems Analysis' (SARSA) and focuses on three principal themes: land settlement, management of natural resources and rural/urban dynamics. To date, SARSA has been involved in research and planning efforts in some twenty countries in Africa, Asia, the Near East, Latin America and the Caribbean; has nearly 100 publications in print or in preparation; and has conducted over a dozen training programs and scholarly meetings.

Under the rural/urban dynamics theme SARSA has concentrated on the roles of settlement schemes, from secondary cities to market towns, in rural regional development. As research progressed on this theme, it became clear that Israeli planners have had considerable experience in settlement planning in rural regions, both in Israel and in the Third World. Moreover, Israeli researchers have tracked the progress of development in rural regions over long periods of time, and their work has many insights to offer concerning changing functional and spatial relationships among settlements as rural regions develop.

The preeminent institution in Israel dealing with rural/urban dynamics in research, planning and training contexts is the Settlement Study Centre (SSC) at Rehovot. Since its inception in 1962, the SSC has been conducting a consistently vigorous research program, has trained about 2,000 post-graduate students from over 50 developing countries in regional planning, has been involved in regional planning exercises in over 40 rural regions in the Third World, and has produced an extensive set of books, working papers and research reports on various subjects related to rural regional development.

In April 1984, a symposium was held at the SSC that brought SARSA and SSC experts together to share experience and research findings, and to explore areas of complementarity. The seminar focused on three primary topics within the context of rural/urban dynamics: the 'Rehovot Approach' to rural regional settlement and development, improving the performance of development planning as a vehicle for guided investment strategies, and the relationships between planned development strategies and implementation strategies. The proceedings of that seminar, under the title 'Rural/Urban Dynamics in Developing Rural Regions', were published in the SARSA publication series. One important conclusion of the seminar was that SARSA and the SSC have much to offer each other, and that a further seminar, more tightly focused on a particular aspect of rural regional development of concern to both institutions, should be organized. In October 14-16, 1985, experts from SARSA and the SSC met in Luxembourg (1) to discuss patterns of change in developing rural regions. Six members from each institution delivered presentations within a prescribed framework on topics reflected in their respective contributions to this volume.

This volume does not, however, represent 'proceedings' in the usual sense. For the formal presentation of each participant was brief, and meant to be but a summary of recent work and findings intended to stimulate discussion. The links and complimentarities among the presentations were explored at length, in both working groups and in plenary sessions. From this emerged a framework for addressing patterns of change in developing rural regions that was somewhat different from the one originally laid out by the seminar organizers. Within that framework, sets of statements concerning individual subjects were articulated, based on the main points of each presentation. Participants were asked over the following few weeks to write up the substance of their presentations in a manner consistent with the new framework and its content. This volume, then, represents findings of the second SARSA/SSC seminar as elaborated by each of the seminar participants from the unique perspective of his or her area of professional specialization.

Scholars, practitioners and policy makers involved in rural regional development seem insufficiently aware of the fact that each individual region has its own unique and dynamic character, and that the roles and functions of towns are essential to that character no less than the nature of agricultural activity. This observation emerged as the fundamental issue of concern to participants in the second SARSA/SSC seminar. At first it might seem that there are two separate subjects involved: rural regions as unique and changing organisms, and the urban aspect of rural development. But the two are in fact one, for it is the lack of recognition of the central roles of towns and cities in rural development that obscures for many the unique and dynamic natures of rural regions.

Changes take place with or without development intervention. In terms of regional analysis, there is a pressing need to understand the changing nature of rural regions, the principal agents of change and the factors involved in their operation, and to incorporate that understanding into the design of development strategies. Rural regional development strategies need to intervene in processes rather than focus on products, to attend explicitly to the non-farm aspects of rural development, and to account for the fact that land, labor, water and technology by themselves do not lead to agricultural development, and certainly not to rural regional development. Employment opportunities and new enterprises in towns are also important.

This volume represents an attempt to articulate the needs and to address them. It suggests analytical approaches to rural regional development that account for the unique and dynamic processes as they exist among farms and towns in the region, and that incorporate a wide variety of elements, especially in the 'urban space' of rural regions, that have a major impact on rural regional economy: markets, towns services, industry and organizations. It also describes related strategic approaches to rural regional development that aim at improving processes of rural regional development.

The volume is divided into five parts. Part One provides an overall conceptual framework for rural regional diagnosis and a strategy design for development intervention. In presenting his framework, Bendavid-Val argues that in order to understand the dynamics of rural regional economies in developing countries we need an approach that integrates behavioural and spatial dynamics, is oriented to current priority development objectives, and focuses on specific dominant commodities produced in the region. The latter are addressed in terms of the means, motivators and markets for their production.

Part Two takes a closer look at the 'urban aspect of rural development'. To set the stage, Rondinelli discusses the roles of towns and cities in rural regional development. This paper describes the expanding variety, complexity, scale and interconnectedness of urban economic and social functions that are needed to meet the changing requirements of agricultural production and marketing as rural regional economies undergo increasing commercialization. If these requirements are not met, rural development cannot proceed. Hence, Rondinelli argues, rural development strategies must account explicitly for the size and distribution of urban settlements, the functions they perform and the linkages among them and the agricultural areas.

McNulty then examines urban-urban relations in the rural regional context. His paper first reviews the consequences of colonial and post-colonial policies for urban systems in developing countries, noting that 'urban systems emerge to serve specific economic, social and political purposes.' He concludes that these policies have been detrimental to the emergence of secondary cities and market towns. The high costs of resultant rural inefficiencies have been born by rural and urban residents alike. McNulty examines the requisites for promoting a well-integrated system of settlements in which rural-urban relations will be characterized by functional complementarity that supports development of both rural and urban areas.

Next, Karaska and Belsky review the 'urban functions in rural development' approach to rural regions, and introduce a new marketing-oriented approach. They distinguish three principal marketing functions performed by rural regional settlement systems: local marketing of goods imported to the region; local marketing of goods produced in the region; and marketing of locally produced goods, mostly agricultural commodities, in markets outside the region. Each marketing system has different spatial manifestations, and their patterns change as regional development proceeds. Interventions in these systems can produce substantial benefits for rural regional development, but must be approached with great care so as not to disrupt existing systems of marketing transactions that are well-suited to local circumstances.

The last article in Part two explores types, applications and benefits of spatial analysis toward rural development planning, and illustrates them with case studies. Painter concludes that spatial policies aimed at strengthening rural/urban relationships offer great regional development potential. He warns us, however, that such relationships do not always benefit both rural and urban residents, and seldom do they benefit both to the same extent. Urban interventions in rural regions must be accompanied by national policies to improve conditions for smallholders in order to avoid reinforcing rural-urban terms of trade that discourage increased agricultural productivity.

Access to rural/regional services, such as health, education, extension, marketing, credit, etc., is a necessary condition for any development, and Part Three deals with that issue. Rushton's chapter concentrates on health services. He describes their evolving patterns in rural regions and analyses the main issues related to their development and to the selection of adequate interventions. Rushton finds that the predominant pattern of change has involved 'the move from urban, hospital-based curative services to small health units, located to maximize geographical accessibility, emphasizing health promotion and disease prevention programs and relying on extensive involvement of the community'. In addition to the growing importance of local organizations, he indicates the importance of interventions that seek to change social conditions that influence health.

Prion follows with a chapter suggesting a method of analysis for the economic evaluation of public services. The common method used in the planning of public services in developing countries is the so-called 'normative planning' method (based on recommended confined norms). The 'operational feasibility analysis' suggested by Prion substitutes 'normative planning' with an economic method that facilitates the estimation of quantities and standards of services on the basis of planned development indicators in the area (instead of fixed predetermined norms).

Part Four relates to one of the most important characteristics of growth, namely the decrease in the relative weight of agriculture in rural employment, and the increase in industrial activities. Bar-El states as a basic assumption that the planning of industrial development in rural areas cannot follow any standard pattern. He analyses the dependence of such a planning process on the specific features of the region and on the surrounding economic structure. Furthermore, he assumes that the attributes of the region change during the process of development, causing a continuous transformation of the relative weights of the various objectives that industrialization is expected to achieve, and of the conditions in which industrialization operates. As a result, no rigid industrial planning can be valid for long. Rather, plans should be prepared on a dynamic basis, taking into consideration the changing industrial structure which would be most adequate to the changing regional typologies at different levels of development. The most important variables that should be considered in the process of industrial planning are indicated, and a few specific hypotheses regarding relations between industrial and regional or national characteristics are suggested.

Schwartz, in her chapter, examines ways of promoting industrial activities. She analyses the role of government in attracting private investment, and focuses on the spatial aspects of directing industrial investment from urban centers to less developed areas. The main types of direct financial incentives in various countries are reviewed. An analysis of the impact of existing policies leads to the conclusion that the direct financial incentives offered to firms willing to locate in specified development areas do not effectively fulfill policy makers' objectives. Often they even cause instability in the region, and by themselves are not enough to encourage investment and economic growth in underdeveloped regions. A successful industrial development policy must include a combination of the various strategies which are available to development authorities, weighted according to the level of development in the region.

Part Five deals with organizational factors in rural regional development. Margulies attributes the lack of development in many regions to the fact that they have only little political power due to the centralization of the decision-making process. She suggests a 'negotiated order' approach to regional development, in which regional development strategy would focus on the relation between the focal region and its environment on the one hand, and the national center on the other. The growth potential of a region would be increased by improving its 'bargaining' position, which is defined as a function of various factors, such as the geopolitical and economic potential and its possible contribution to national growth; the electoral political potential; the extent of regional, physical and social organizations, etc.

Sherman's discussion of the development of agency-villager relations attempts to place the analysis of this specific topic within the broader framework of differing basic approaches to the definition of the 'development' character of development administration. Two schools are identified: administrative ecology and administrative engineering, and their implications for analysis of field operations in rural areas are discussed. The author proposes new approaches to the questions examined: policy implementation and social engineering.

The last chapter describes the framework of organization for cooperation within the rural sector, the changes which may occur in this framework in the process of development and some of the spatial implications of the organizational framework. Wilkansky deals with the process of building an effective organizational supporting framework for rural development. One major conclusion concerns the need for an articulated multi-level system with horizontal and vertical linkages in order to ensure a stable and orderly development. Another major conclusion relates to the need to strengthen the simultaneous and integrated organizational development of the rural and the urban sectors.

NOTES

1. We wish to acknowledge the support of Clark University and the Institut Superieur d'Etudes et des Recherches Pedagogiques, Walferdange, Luxembourg.

Part 1: Assessing Rural Regional Patterns

MEANS, MOTIVATORS AND MARKETS IN RURAL REGIONAL DEVELOPMENT

Avrom Bendavid-Val

What is needed now is a greater readiness to step outside one's own discipline to look afresh at the validity to the African development situation of premises underlying specific disciplines... The predominant paradigms do not yet point to the roots of the problems (in Africa).

Goren Hyden (1)

INTRODUCTION

There is a renewed concern with development of subnational regions, and particularly with rural regional development, among developing countries and donor agencies. In many of these, after a period of designating development regions, setting up regional development authorities and launching regional development programs in the later 1960s and early 1970s, enthusiasm waned. This happened because the institutional machinery for regional development did not work, because the accomplishments of region-based development programs failed or because priorities had to be shifted for other reasons. In some agencies regional development was so often associated with integrated rural development schemes that failed, that until recently one could not even suggest it as a serious basis for planning development interventions. Recently, however, quite a number of USAID Missions and their corresponding Regional Bureaus in Washington, have begun to engage in regional development endeavors, though only occasionally do the endeavors go by that name.(2) This is particularly true in AID's Asia/Near East Region and in its Africa Region, where regional development activities are under way in the Philippines, Indonesia, Jordan, Tunisia, Togo, Zaire and Somalia, to name but a few cases. The same trend, if not yet everywhere as pronounced, can be detected in the programs, research agendas and conference topics of other donor and development research organizations, as well as in the five-year plan statements of developing countries.

To some extent, this new or renewed concern derives from a growing awareness of the need to address urban development problems in developing countries. Looking at things urban beyond housing and the massive urban deficits in metropolitan areas, one quickly notices networks of secondary cities and lower-order towns. These urban settings have characteristics rather different from those of metropolitan areas, and many of the economic activities that go on within them are linked to what transpires in their rural hinterlands. This means that development in those cities and towns is not likely to take place on a sustained basis if it does not also occur in their hinterlands.(3) And this, in turn, suggests the idea of regional development.

Whatever its origin, the growing concern with rural regional development is welcome. Development strategies that address territorially defined subareas of a country from the multisectoral perspective have long been believed by many to be essential to any viable approach to sustainable national development. Some would argue that the overwhelming metropolitan problems of developing countries, the persistent food deficits, the intractable foreign exchange problems, and even the crisis in development administration, can all be traced in material degree to development policies that did not account for specific needs of specific regions of the country. Ultimately, a developing national economy means a nation of developing regional economies. It therefore makes sense to concentrate a substantial portion of development resources on measures to strengthen those regional economies.

Pursuit of rural regional development has several implications. Conceptually, it implies strengthening the economies of territorially defined nonmetropolitan areas within a country; concentrating on specific population groups and activities within those regions; building on intersectoral, rural/urban and urban/urban functional relationships within those regions and between each of them and other regions of the country; and organizing institutional relationships and capacities that connect regional development planning with national development planning on the one hand, and with local development planning on the other. In terms of policy, it means formulating macropolicy in a way that is designed to strengthen rural regional economies; formulating regional development policy specific to the needs of each region; and coordinating the use of policy implementation tools - public investment and service provision, regulation, economic incentives and disincentives, information, and public procurement - for targeted purposes within each region.

But there is no generally applicable way of going about the regional development planning process, by means of which the distance from broad concept to specific development policy for a particular region is transversed. The planning process in any particular case reflects circumstances and priority development objectives unique to the region at the time. However, credible development planning process entails, one way or another, a diagnosis of the regional situation and a formulation of intervention strategies based on that diagnosis.

Strong connection exists between regional diagnosis and regional development intervention strategies, because the approach used to study the region - the overriding questions addressed, the data collected, the techniques used to analyze basic data - largely determines the intervention strategies that will be formulated. The nature of possible intervention strategies, on the other hand, determines the information needed to inform their design. Hence, regional diagnosis and design of regional development intervention strategies take place within a more-or-less consistent conceptual framework, though often the conceptual framework is implicit rather than explicit.

The conceptual framework is a broad model, made up of notions concerning the key elements in a regional economy and the key relationships that occur among them. Regional diagnosis examines those elements and relationships, and intervention strategies are designed to alter them. The conceptual framework for diagnosis and intervention also influences the organizations and individuals that participate in rural regional planning, because it determines the technical capabilities needed for regional diagnosis and the policy implementation authorities needed to carry out intervention strategies. A guiding conceptual framework for rural regional development thus constitutes an essential structure for a cohesive regional planning process.

In the following pages we describe a particular conceptual framework for rural regional development, and discuss some of its implications. This conceptual framework, or guiding 'model,' was devised for regional planning endeavors in which the priority development objectives are to increase agricultural productivity on the farms and to expand income-earning opportunities in the towns. It is presented here because these are priority objectives in many current efforts of rural regional planning, and so its relevance may be broad. Moreover, the framework is unusual in its explicit integration of behavioral and spatial dynamics in rural regional development, and this may be of interest to students of regional development planning.

A CONCEPTUAL FRAMEWORK FOR RURAL REGIONAL DEVELOPMENT

The conceptual framework described below was developed within the context of specific operative circumstances and requirements while working with AID in Sub-Sahara Africa. The most important of these are:

1. In Sub-Sahara Africa, AID has been concerned with the alarming decline in per capita food production and the explosive rate of urban population growth; hence the priority objectives of expanding agricultural productivity and urban income opportunities.
   income

2. USAID Missions in African countries have been looking for approaches to urban development problems, but generally are not equipped to make radical

departures from their traditional planning which is oriented to rural development. These approaches, therefore, should enable them to build on past and current agricultural and rural development activity, and on existing planning expertise.

3. Sought especially is an approach to the planning or rural regional development interventions that will lead to improved productivity of existing farmers on their farms.

4. Rural regional development planning, while accounting for town as well as farm activity, cannot be comprehensive. Funding, skills, and administrative capacity all are limited. The emphasis must therefore be on relatively modest interventions aimed at achieving the priority objectives and at fostering regional dynamics that sustain the improvement.

5. The economies of many rural regions in Sub-Sahara Africa are largely dependent upon a small number of dominant crops or groups of related crops. That is, most economic activity in a rural region is associated directly or indirectly with the growing and selling of those crops, or with the spending of income earned from them.

This context reflects the situation among many donor organizations and rural regions of developing countries on all continents. Moreover, even in ostensibly different rural regional contexts, such as irrigation and settlement schemes, many of the operative circumstances and requirements are similar. For example, skills and administrative capacity are limited and concentrated in agricultural and rural development; funds are scarce, and investments beyond the basic settlement infrastructure need to be relatively modest; initial economic viability of settlement in both rural and rurban areas is dependent upon a few dominant crops or crop types.

In looking for a conceptual framework to guide the diagnosis and formulation of rural regional development intervention strategies in specific regions in several African countries, we reviewed existing models of rural and regional development. Though valid elements were readily found in them, existing models tended to rest either on implicit assumptions about the spatial context,(4) or on implicit assumptions about the behavioral context.(5) The few exceptions (6) were highly formulaic and comprehensive, and were simply unsuited to the situation at hand.

What was needed was a guide to facilitate and motivate farm production in a given region, and a clue to the links of these two to urban enterprise in the region's towns. The conceptual framework had to encompass both the behavioral dynamics of agricultural productivity and the associated spatial dynamics of farm/town relationships. Rather than approach the region from the perspective of traditional economic sectors, agricultural development, or urban development, we need to understand all three as elements in the facilitating and motivating of agricultural production in the region.

Below is a scheme representing the emerging conceptual framework in its simplest terms.

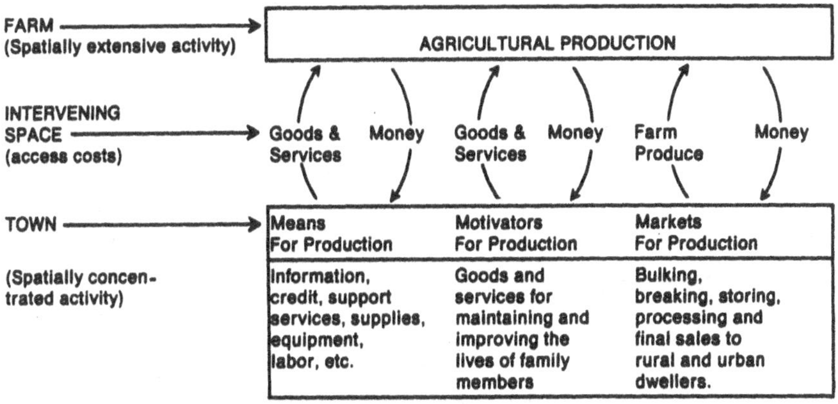

The scheme is based on the observation that maintaining and increasing the productivity of farmers on their farms requires, in addition to water: ***means*** for production, including information, credit, support services, supplies such as seed and fertilizers, equipment, perhaps labour, and the like; ***motivators*** for production, including most commonly the goods and services for maintaining and improving the lives of farm family members; ***markets*** for farm produce, through which farm families earn the income (or are able to obtain credit) to acquire the means and motivating goods and services for continuing and expanding production.

The means, motivators and markets for agricultural production are, for the most part, town-based. Means and motivators are generally obtained in or through towns and cities, and in many cases are produced there. The output markets, whether for local final sales, national markets, processing, or even export sales, also operate through towns and cities.(7) Moreover, provision of means, motivators and markets for agricultural production is the principal basis for urban employment and enterprise opportunities, especially in smaller towns and cities.(8)

The sustaining and increasing of agricultural productivity and the promoting of off-farm employment and enterprise opportunities are therefore intimately associated in rural regional development and in national development. Availability of means, motivators and markets for agricultural production is as essential for increasing agricultural productivity as water and improved production technologies. Agricultural production systems incorporating town-based elements in the region are as important for fostering off-farm employment and enterprise opportunities as credit and management skills.

To translate the scheme into a conceptual framework that can be useful for a specific rural region, 'farms' and 'towns' should be taken as representing networks of places; 'agricultural production' should be taken as referring to a particular dominant or representative agricultural commodity; means, motivators and markets would be those associated with the particular commodity. The scheme thus becomes a framework for an examination of the operations of 'production systems' for a specific dominant or representative agricultural commodity in the region. The term 'production system' as used here encompasses the four major components reflected in the scheme.

One could imagine a map of the region illustrating the important elements of production activity, provision of means, provision of motivators and marketing for the production system of a particular agricultural commodity. Elements of the production system would be represented on the map in qualitative, quantitative and spatial terms. Conceptually, 'overlays' of these maps combine to portray aggregate activities, such as agricultural marketing, input supply, transportation services and so on, at and among rural and urban locations in the region.(9)

RURAL REGIONAL DIAGNOSIS

What approach does the above "3-M production system" conceptual framework suggest for regional diagnosis? Data on aggregate activities in and among various locations in the regions would be accumulated from information about the operations of individual commodity production systems. This means that data on aggregate activities would be incomplete. For example, the estimated volume of trade in agricultural produce at a particular market center would be the sum of trade recorded only for the commodities selected for study. These commodities, however, would be the dominant and representative ones.

From the 3-M perspective, interest in the market center would be aimed at its role in the production systems of those commodities. The 3-M production system framework guides regional diagnosis toward a limited analysis of the region. The approach is to study in depth a few key components of the regional economy, namely the production system of dominant agricultural commodities or commodity groups. The purpose of regional analysis is to inform the design of the desirable development interventions. Intervention strategies will then be formulated around specific commodity production systems and aim at improving productivity, efficiency, market mechanisms and regional multipliers within them.

The first task is to select the commodity production systems to be studied. Some preliminary analysis may be required to determine which commodities dominate or represent agriculture in the region, but this knowledge is most often readily at hand. Seldom will the commodity production systems that ought to be studied in a given rural region number more than six. These should be selected so as to allow an assessment of different types of commodities, production and market orientations which are of significance in the region. Among the selected commodities we might find items that are produced primarily: for export markets, for regional markets, for domestic national markets, by small-holders, and/or on plantations, state farms or large private farms.

While the conceptual framework derives from an overriding concern with agricultural production, the same spatially disaggregated production system framework can be employed for urban-based or rural nonagricultural products, such as manufactured goods, charcoal or minerals mined in the region. It is simply a matter of documenting spatial expression of the production activity, provision of means and motivators and marketing for a specific commodity.

In the Lower Juba Valley of Somalia, where the 3-M framework is being used, the commodities selected for study were livestock and associated products, bananas, maize and machine maintenance and repair. Livestock is the dominant commodity in the region and a major source of export and domestic food. The extent to which this nomadic production activity is linked to the towns of the region in terms of inputs, motivators and final markets has not been documented. It is being studied because we do not know how it actually serves and is served by the regional economy.

Bananas are also a dominant export-oriented commodity. It is a plantation crop produced by large private landholders and government enterprises. The sources of means (except field labor), the motivators and the markets for this commodity are chiefly outside the regional economy. Maize is a staple crop produced principally by smallholders. The trade in this commodity in regional markets is brisk and large quantities are marketed outside the region. Other major, though not dominant, agricultural commodities produced in the region have similar characteristics.

Machine maintenance and repair was selected as an urban activity. In this case, information relating only to the three agricultural commodities under study is not enough, because machine maintenance and repair services are likely to be critical to any expansion in agricultural productivity. However, their available quantity and quality at various locations in the region is likely to be significantly influenced, at least in the intermediate term, by factors which are not related to the production systems for livestock, bananas or maize. In other words, the strategic role of this 'commodity' in development requires that its 'production system' be fully understood in order to design realistic and effective intervention strategies.

The four components of a production system must now be translated into categories of information to be documented. There is a number of possible approaches to this, depending on the nature of the rural region in question and the research resources available. If a relatively comprehensive approach is possible, the following information might be collected for each commodity production system:

1. ***Production***. Technologies employed, quantities produced, costs, cycles of production, market signal responses, decision-makers, provision of labor, sites of various phases of production, use of working capital etc.

2. ***Inputs***. Types, quantities, costs, means of acquisition and sources of means of production, location of technical information, credit, support services (including legal, administrative and security), supplies, equipment, labor etc.

3. ***Use of Revenues*** (for acquiring, or not acquiring, means and motivators of production). Actual and desired types, quantities and locations of savings, repair/replacement investment, growth investment, outside investment, taxes, fees, government revenues, remittances, other transfers, production credit interest and principal, consumer credit interest and principal, producer and consumer goods and services purchases, and other outlays in relation to revenues.

4. ***Marketing*** (process of acquisition of income for obtaining means and motivators of production). Transportation, physical facilities, distribution

(breaking, bulking, storing), processing, labor, institutions, seasons, locations, price signal, contract and other aspects of the marketing system.

In practice this list would naturally be refined to suit circumstances, and the regional analysis would be performed at a level of detail determined by need and resources. However, if we want the information, even anecdotal information, to be useful for the design of intervention strategies which are consistent with the 3-M conceptual framework, it must, as the list suggests, be tied to specific locations. The implications of this may go beyond what at first appears to be the case. On the farm side, for example, there may be different production patterns for significant types or sizes of farms that produce the same commodity. On the town side, access by farmers to means, motivators and markets may be only the last event in a sequence of transactions predominantly among towns; and these urban/urban relationships may have to be traced in order to document rural/urban dynamics in the region as they really are.

This is not the place to explore ways of collecting, processing and displaying information on individual commodity production systems or aggregate functions in the region. But the 3-M framework does have broad implications for these activities, as any conceptual framework should. For example, since commodity production systems are multisectoral, their analysis must be multidisciplinary. The skills that may be required involve not only specialists in regional analysis, but also anthropologists, ecologists, experts in agricultural systems, knowledge of local history, culture and institutions, marketing specialists, small business specialists and others, depending upon the situation. People who live and work in the region must participate in the assessment as collectors of information and as valuable sources of information and of guidance regarding the most pertinent information.

Moreover, the 3-M framework suggests an accumulation of behavioral, spatial and economic information through labor-intensive method of primary data collection at specific places. Therefore, unless research resources are extensive specific items to be documented must be chosen with care. But in order to know which elements of a commodity production system most warrant detailed study, we must first know how that system works, which implies a two-stage analysis process.

The first stage entails sufficient field observations, interviews and statistical research to enable reasonable definition of each commodity production system as it operates in the region. Quantification in the first stage may amount to no more than rough estimates of relative orders of magnitude, associated with functions and linkages among the various locations in the region that play a significant role in each system. The second stage involves more detailed collection and analysis of data for elements of each system selected for further study. Functions and linkages may be selected for detailed study because of their significance within a particular commodity production system or for the commodity production systems in aggregate, or because of their potential significance for interventions to alter a commodity production system.

DESIGNING INTERVENTION STRATEGIES

As mentioned earlier, the 3-M production system conceptual framework guides regional diagnosis, or analysis, so that it informs the design of intervention strategies built around specific regional commodity production systems. These strategies would be made up of coordinated direct and indirect interventions in production activity, provision of means and motivators, and/or marketing components of each production system. They would be aimed at increasing agricultural productivity in the region through a process that expands private employment and enterprise opportunities in the towns. It is easy to see the basis for cohesiveness in the planning process that is provided by the conceptual framework.

The 3-M framework focuses diagnosis, and therefore policy and project interventions, on rural regional dynamics, namely on the systemic relationships among things. It is a process-oriented framework by means of which production endeavors are examined as multifaceted multisectoral processes involving many groups and locations that function interdependently. Derivative intervention strategies may be incremental, but the activities within them are easily coordinated and designed to reinforce each other. Mistakes such as improving the marketing systems but ignoring access to means and motivations of production, or providing better production technologies but overlooking the marketing improvements required to accommodate increased output, could be avoided by a diagnosis based on the 3-M production system framework.

In fact, diagnosis and design of intervention strategies may be undertaken simultaneously. For example, the first stage analysis may reveal that in aggregate, the most critical obstacles to increased agricultural production are the high cost of water pumps and the unavailability of parts and repair services (access to means of production), the unavailability of high school education for farm children (the ability to pay for which would be a powerful motivator for increased production), and a high spoilage rate owing to inadequate storage facilities for marketing produce (limited output markets). The second stage of the regional diagnosis, which involves a detailed study, may be designed to determine precisely what types of interventions would be most effective and where.

In any particular rural region there may be "sectoral programs" deriving neither from a careful order of priorities of development objectives, nor from a broad diagnosis of the regional economy. There may be a drive to expand the access of health care facilities in rural areas, for example, to strengthen infrastructure and public services in rural towns, to promote rural industrialization, to expand irrigation in a portion of the countryside, or to improve produce market facilities in market towns. Such programs can be initiated in many ways - independent determinations of needs, availability of particular donor programs, political necessity etc., and each entails sectoral diagnosis and design of sectoral intervention strategies.

The 3-M production system framework can be integrated with sectoral studies, and used to orient sectoral intervention strategies toward priority objectives of regional economic development. With regard to health care, for example, knowledge based on the 3-M production system analysis can help determine what types of health care facilities will have the greatest impact on agricultural productivity and where. With regard to strengthening the infrastructure and public services in towns, an analysis based on 3-M might complement urban function scalogram and related analyses to determine which urban facilities, if improved, are likely to improve the operation of key agricultural commodity production systems. An analysis of an irrigation system based on 3-M may suggest complementary investments for the provision of means, motivators and markets for production that will maximize regional development benefits.

The 3-M production system framework can also serve as an intellectual tool for designing sectoral or other special studies in a way that will help those studies inform the design of intervention strategies for priority objectives of rural regional development. As an illustration, consider the subject of remittances that has been studied intensively in recent years. There is much that could be studied about remittances, or receipts from other non-farm activities, in rural regions. But if we wish to concentrate resources on aspects that are most relevant to regional agricultural productivity and associated town-based activities, the 3-M framework suggests the following research questions: do town-to-farm remittances (or receipts from other non-farm activities) diminish the incentive effects of motivators for agricultural production? Do they diminish the need for motivators of production? Do they alter rural tastes and needs so as to change the motivational attributes of potential motivators? Do they increase access to means of agricultural production? How do they influence rural/urban interaction? Is the ability to make farm-to-town remittances, to support a kin in the city, a motivator for agricultural production?

If we are dealing with urban development, the most appropriate questions are: in what ways are the economies of rural regional towns and cities tied to specific agricultural production systems in the region, both directly and indirectly? In what ways could they be linked better? What sorts of urban investments would enhance national and regional economies by increasing the productivity efficiency and multipliers of specific rural commodity production systems? What functions and commodity systems offer the greatest opportunities for employment and small enterprises? How do various rural towns function as sites of production, output markets, sources of consumer goods and services and sources of inputs?

Or, with regard to macropolicy reviews: what are the consequences of tariff, foreign exchange and agricultural pricing policies on access to means and motivators of production? What are the effects of agricultural export policies on the viability of local agricultural marketing systems? In what ways do urban investment policies support or undermine the availability of means, motivators and markets in key rural regional commodity production systems? In what way do parastatal operations supplant or support the functions of regional towns and cities in providing means, motivators and markets for agricultural production?

For those concerned with the development of institutions, the 3-M production system framework would help determine the order of priorities for strengthening rural institutions. For those concerned with beneficiary self-empowerment process, it would provide a basis for identifying potentials for coalition building and for cooperative decision-making and advocacy work. For those concerned with welfare, specifically of the rural poor, it would help target assistance through economic activities in which the poor are - or could be - engaged. For those concerned with participatory analysis and planning, it would provide a framework for beneficiary assembly and analysis of information, and a guide to planning process procedures. For those concerned with agricultural technology, it would provide insights into complementary urban-based activities essential for the success of technological innovation. For those concerned with sociocultural determinants of rural behavior, it would provide a framework for organizing observations and translating them into information that is useful for decision makers.

The 3-M production system conceptual framework can help weave diverse threads of the rural regional fabric into a behavioral and spatial dynamics that can bring about production and distribution of principal regional commodities.

NOTES

1. See the Introduction to Hyden (1983) for further elaboration.

2. These activities may go by names such as river basin or river valley development, provincial development, area development, irrigated perimeter development, decentralized development, or secondary city/market town and periphery development. What places them all in the category of rural regional development is their focus on multisectoral economic development in particular regions of nonmetropolitan national territory that include both urban and rural areas.

3. Excellent discussions concerning the roles of small cities and the rural context of urban development will be found in Gibb (1984), Mathur (1982), Rondinelli (1983), Rondinelli and Ruddle (1978), and Wanmali (1982).

4. A good example will be found in the well-known work by Mellor (1966).

5. A good example, with reference to other well-known spatial models, will be found in the recent book by Rondinelli (1985).

6. Good examples will be found in Johnson (1970) and Weitz (1971).

7. In some cases, 'towns' may be embryonic, taking the form of periodic rural markets. Historically, with an expanding regional economy these markets tend to evolve into settled urban communities.

8. This holds whether markets and enterprises are run by private entrepreneurs, community groups, communes, cooperatives, municipalities, provinces or national governments.

9. Many constructs that were put forward by other authors are related to the one presented here. For example, Mosher (1966) refers to five factors that affect the pace of agricultural development: markets for farm products, changing technology, local availability of supplies and equipment, production incentives for farmers and transportation. There are, of course, many ways to categorize the elements of an 'agricultural production system'. What distinguishes the conceptual framework put forth here from others that may include the same elements is that it incorporates those elements in a unified framework of be-

havioral and spatial dynamics, and considers them with respect to specific commodities.

REFERENCES

Gibb, A. "Tertiary Urbanization: The Agricultural Market as a Consumption Related Phenomenon," *Regional Development Dialogue*. Nagoya: United Nations Centre for Regional Development, 1984.

Hazell, P., and Roell, A. *Rural Growth Linkages: Household Expenditure Patterns in Malaysia and Nigeria*. Washington, DC: International Food Policy Research Institute, 1983.

Hyden, G. *No Shortcuts to Progress: African Development Management in Perspective*. Berkeley: University of California Press, 1983.

Johnson, E.A.J. *The Organization of Space in Developing Countries*. Cambridge: Harvard University Press, 1970.

Mathur, Om (ed.). *Small Cities and National Development*. Nagoya: United Nations Centre for Regional Development, 1982.

Mellor, J. *The economics of Agricultural Development*. Ithaca: Cornell University Press, 1966.

Mosher, A. *Getting Agriculture Moving*. New York: Praeger, 1966.

Rondinelli, D. *Secondary Cities in Developing Countries*. Beverly Hills: Sage Publications, 1983.

---------. *Applied Methods of Regional Analysis: The Spatial Dimensions of Development Policy*. Boulder: Westview Press, 1985.

Rondinelli, D., and Ruddle, K. *Urbanization and Rural Development: A Spatial Policy for Equitable Growth*. New York: Praeger, 1978.

Wanmali, S. *Service Provision and Rural Development in India: A Study of Miryalguda Taluka*. Washington, DC: International Food Policy Research Institute, 1982.

Weitz, R. *From Peasant to Farmer*. New York: Columbia University Press, 1971.

Part 2: Rural/Urban Dynamics

ROLES OF TOWNS AND CITIES IN THE DEVELOPMENT OF RURAL REGIONS

Dennis A. Rondinelli

As a region develops from a subsistence or low-surplus agricultural economy to one that is more commercialized or diversified, the requirements for increasing agricultural output become more numerous and complex. As a region begins producing a traded surplus rather than simply providing for the consumption needs of rural households, new production inputs, supporting services, infrastructure, marketing outlets and commercial organizations must be available to maintain higher levels of production and ensure a steady economic return to the regional economy. In addition, new and more dynamic physical and economic linkages must be forged between rural areas, towns and cities. Urban centers ranging from market towns with a population of 15,000 to 20,000 or more, small cities of 30,000 to 100,000 residents and secondary cities with 100,000 to over a million inhabitants come to play a vital role in regional development. They are especially important as markets for agricultural goods, as sources of agricultural and commercial inputs and as centers of off-farm employment. Physical and economic linkages between rural areas and urban centers and among towns and cities in a region begin to play a crucial role in facilitating the dynamic relationships that allow a regional economy to grow and diversity, and in influencing the distribution of income from agricultural development.

This paper examines the changes that occur in regions in transition from a subsistence or low-surplus agricultural economy to a commercial and more diversified one. It focuses particularly on essential factors to increased agricultural productivity and the roles of cities and towns in regional development.

FACTORS AFFECTING AGRICULTURAL DEVELOPMENT

In nearly every developing country, five factors affect the pace of agricultural development: markets for farm products, changing technology, local availability of supplies and equipment, production incentives for farmers and transportation (Mosher, 1955). Some of these factors can be provided by the farmers themselves through cooperative efforts; others must be provided by private entrepreneurs in response to growing demand, by local and national governments concerned with accelerating agricultural production and rural development, or by some combination of public and private investment. But weaknesses in rural market mechanisms and organizational structures in poor regions often require governments to play an important role, at least initially, in creating these factors and in extending access to them.

As demand for food increases and production expands beyond the subsistence level, agricultural output depends on a larger constellation of inputs and supporting services that, together, form the region's farming system. Studies of developing countries have shown that the elements of the system usually include the following (Hopgood and Millikan, 1965; Mellor, 1967; Wharton, 1969):

1. ***Physical Input Factors.*** Seeds, water, natural or commercial fertilizers and pesticides, work animals or farm machinery, manufactured tools and human labor.

2. ***Economic Factors.*** Transport, storage, processing and marketing facilities for farm products; facilities for the supply and distribution of inputs, including credit; affordable input prices; favorable product prices; and appropriate agricultural tax and subsidy policies.

3. ***Organizational Factors.*** Favorable land tenure arrangements; public policies supporting agricultural development; farmers' organizations that can coordinate physical inputs; economic, social and public services needed by rural households.

4. ***Knowledge Factors.*** Effective organization of basic and applied agricultural research and diffusion of knowledge relating to technology, economic factors, farming methods and agricultural policy.

The entire structure of the agricultural economy in a region changes as production increases and farming becomes more commercialized (Johnston and Kilby, 1975). Technical and managerial efficiency must be increased through the adoption of technological innovations, and inputs must be combined more effectively. Larger inputs of land and labor are usually needed. Pressures increase for bringing new land into cultivation or extending the growing period on existing land. At the same time, the need for capital inputs also increases. Production is expanded initially through the use of nonwage farm labor, later through the application of biological and chemical inputs, and finally through the use of labor-saving technology. New demands and opportunities arise for agricultural research, for extension and education programs, and for modification in local and national political, institutional and economic structures that affect attitudes, perceptions and values.

Structural changes in the agricultural economy of a region are usually bound up with economic changes in other sectors. Rising per capita income not only stimulates demand for food, but also shifts the types of foods demanded from staple grains and starches to vegetables, meats, dairy products and fruit. Meeting the demands for these commercial crops requires inputs from the transport, service, manufacturing and commercial sectors, and increased investment by government in infrastructure and utilities.

Once the demand for food increases, the capacity of farm households to expand production and raise their incomes also depends on their access to an efficient marketing system. Farmers must be able to get their goods to market quickly and cheaply after harvest, and to store goods that cannot be sold at a favorable price. An effective system of processing contributes to marketing improvements, initially by reducing waste and lowering transport costs. But an efficient processing industry also makes goods available in more convenient forms to consumers, thereby expanding the markets for agricultural products (Abbot, 1967; Mittendorf, 1981).

THE ROLES OF TOWNS AND CITIES IN REGIONAL DEVELOPMENT

As regions are transformed from subsistence to surplus production economies, periodic marketing systems are also transformed and consolidated into commercial marketing systems. Market towns, small cities and large urban centers come to play a crucial role in providing farm inputs and absorbing agricultural products. Under these conditions, as Weitz and his associates have pointed out (1976, p. 6), the location of public and private investments in strategically located towns and cities becomes an essential instrument for accelerating agricultural development. They argue that "agriculture does not develop by itself. It requires a complete institutional system to support it, market its products, and provide inputs, credit and professional advice. The rural community, which is the agent of agricultural development, needs services for its population, such as education, health, public facilities and commercial outlets. The efficiency and location of both producer and consumer services exert a strong influence on the success of agricultural development."

Programs for strengthening the functions of centrally located towns and cities that act as markets and as processing and distribution sites, and provide basic services and facilities for people living in surrounding areas, is one means of maintaining and accelerating the pace of agricultural development in a region.

The primary function of market towns in poor rural regions or in regions undergoing the initial stages of transition from subsistence to commercial agriculture, is to act as consumption and services centers for agricultural households. Indeed, these functions - and presumably the market towns themselves - come into being as the result of agricultural expansion (Gibb, 1984).

As the agricultural economy grows and diversifies, its continued expansion becomes more dependent on the economic and social functions performed by towns and cities (Rondinelli and Ruddle, 1977; Rondinelli, 1983). Where cities and towns function effectively they:

1. Offer institutionalized points of exchange at which farmers can bring their agricultural goods and products to be sold to people who come from a wide area to engage in trade.

2. Serve as distribution centers in which small amounts of agricultural goods can be bulked for distribution and sale in larger markets in other parts of the region or country, and to which mobile traders can bring goods manufactured in larger cities for sale locally.

3. Provide outlets in both the marketplace and in shops and stalls surrounding the market for a wide range of basic consumer goods such as clothing, crafts, household items, cooking utensils, processed food and furniture, as well as farm supplies, implements, fertilizers and other inputs needed to increase agricultural production.

4. Offer a wide range of personal and commercial services such as credit, storage, mills and processing facilities, transportation, brokerage, blacksmithing and repair services, in a convenient location.

5. Provide basic public and social services such as post offices, licensing and registration offices, branch offices of national government agencies, elementary and high schools, vocational schools, maternity and child care services, dispensaries and health clinics, agricultural extension and technical services.

6. Provide a channel through which new ideas, technology or ways of doing things can be introduced into a rural region, and a place where farmers can see them demonstrated or observe the effects of their application.

7. Serve as a focal point for religious, social and recreational activities by providing locations for churches, temples, social organizations, festivals, bars, restaurants and sports competitions.

8. Offer opportunities for off-farm employment in small-scale industry, in commercial and services enterprises and in agro-processing and distribution activities, and provide apprenticeship training in the range of crafts, service and productive activities found in the market center.

As the agricultural economy in a region grows and diversifies, larger cities within the region and metropolitan areas in other regions also provide markets and act as centers of trade for agricultural goods. Urban population growth and agglomeration create increased demand for agricultural products from nearby rural areas; agricultural markets in cities provide employment opportunities for urban workers in a large number of commercial and service activities related to market trade; and the cities function as agricultural supply centers and as locations for agricultural processing and agri-business activities (Rondinelli, 1984). Research indicates that the growth of cities strongly influences agricultural cropping patterns, the intensity of land use and returns to agricultural investment in surrounding areas. In addition, it creates demand for cottage industry goods produced by rural households. In some countries, rapidly increasing agricultural productivity drives people from rural areas to cities in search of new employment and economic opportunities, and the employment of migrants in cities is a source of income remittance to farm households in rural areas (Rondinelli, 1984).

Perhaps the single most important role of cities and towns in agricultural development is that they form the physical structure through which agricultural goods flow from the farm to final markets (Lele, 1971). In early stages of surplus production, marketing chains - the sequence of transactions and commodity movements from producer to consumer - become longer and involve larger numbers of small-scale intermediaries. As agricultural production in rural areas expands to meet urban food needs, the number of market centers usually increases. Periodic markets in some areas begin to expand and meet more frequently, and new markets evolve in the areas between existing ones. The number of goods and services offered in marketplaces increases, and stronger and more numerous intermarket trading linkages evolve. The larger markets attract more traders and intermediaries from a greater distance. Markets in the region begin to form a hierarchy in size, diversity and volume of goods traded (Bromley, 1971).

Typically, goods that are not retained by rural households for consumption, feed, seed or in-kind payments are sold by farmers through cooperatives or town-based itinerant traders, directly to consumers in village marketplaces, to local traders, brokers, truckers or commission agents, or to government marketing agents in nearby towns. Local traders, in turn, sell the goods in town markets to other traders and brokers, or to millers, hullers or processors in small cities. Some of the good are consumed locally in the villages and towns; some are processed and sold to wholesalers from larger cities; and some are resold to government marketing boards and retailers in regional urban centers. Some products are bulked for sale to exporters in large cities, and others find their way through middlemen and brokers to metropolitan areas, where they are sold by wholesalers to grocery stores, supermarkets, restaurants and institutions, and by retailers, hawkers and vendors to individual consumers. People working in the 'informal sector' usually dominate an important part of the food distribution network from producer to seller to consumer in Third World cities (Lam, 1982).

As regional development proceeds, new transport and communication linkages make travel for traders and consumers to larger market centers less expensive and more convenient. Many periodic and small daily markets either disappear or are absorbed by larger ones. Larger and smaller markets become organized in a more definitive hierarchy and are more integrated spatially. Trade interactions tend to increase and the meetings of periodic markets become more synchronized (Bromley, 1971). The marketing chain then tends to shorten again; small-scale mobile traders are increasingly displaced by larger urban-based wholesalers, and farmers have more direct access to market centers.

Thus, towns and cities form the physical structure of marketing through which urban demand absorbs agricultural products. Cities, in turn, depend on agricultural output for their survival and growth. The economies of small towns as well as of larger cities depend on agriculture-related production activities for employment and income.

STRENGTHENING THE ROLES OF CITIES AND TOWNS

Although a good deal of evidence suggests that market centers, towns and cities *can* play important roles in the development of rural regions in many developing countries, the settlement system is neither well developed not integrated sufficiently to facilitate agricultural expansion. Problems arise from three major sources.

First, many rural regions in developing countries lack sufficient numbers of towns and cities of adequate population size to be able to support the wide range of services, facilities, infrastructure and productive activities needed to sustain regional agricultural growth. In many regions the population is scattered widely in settlements of very small size that are neither big enough nor accessible enough to provide these functions efficiently. In others, the market towns and service centers that do exist are not distributed widely enough geographically to allow people living throughout the region to have access to them (Rondinelli, 1983a).

Development planners and policy-makers are now aware that if agricultural productivity and employment opportunities are to be il.employment expanded in rural regions, a well developed and physically integrated system of market towns and cities must serve as the base for regional development. Because of the scarcity of investment resources in most developing countries, many projects that are needed to support agricultural development and off-farm rural enterprises cannot be scattered widely over the countryside. They must be concentrated in strategically located settlements that have adequate populations to support them and are accessible to people living in a large surrounding area.

Second, in many areas where towns and cities do exist, they do not offer many services and facilities or appropriate infrastructure because of inadequate investment. Thus, settlements that might act as market and service centers for their areas do not do so because they lack the appropriate combination of functions that would make them attractive to people who must travel long distances to use them.

Bromley (1984) argues that regional development policies that seek to strengthen the role of market towns in promoting agricultural development must address two major issues. The first is to ensure an optimal distribution of marketing facilities in accessible towns and cities through a region. The second is to assure that the towns and cities in which marketing facilities and services are located are linked to each other in mutually beneficial ways. Bromley identifies several ways in which governments can intervene to improve marketing systems as instruments of regional development: (1) establishing new markets; (2) synchronizing market days; (3) increasing the effectiveness of market regulations; (4) installing complementary services at market sites; (5) providing mobile government services in market centers; (6) providing better market information and publicity; and (7) ensuring that public services located in market towns are kept open on weekend market days. Finally, governments must also undertake policy reforms aimed at increasing the efficiency and effectiveness of agricultural marketing practices.

Third, in some rural regions that do have large numbers of towns, the settlements are not physically and economically integrated. They are not effectively linked to larger urban markets for agricultural products. Nor are linkages between them and their surrounding rural areas strongly developed. Thus, only people living within towns and cities benefit from their services and facilities, while people living in peripheral or distant areas have little or no access to them.

Investments in physical infrastructure and facilities that strengthen the above functions and link towns and cities to rural areas can have a strong impact on accelerating agricultural development and generating increased income for rural households. Recent studies of rural-urban road investments in developing countries, for example, indicate the pervasive impact these linkages can have on agriculture and on a regional economy.

The benefits of these new physical linkages include the following (Anderson and Vandevoort, 1982; Cobb *et al*, 1980; Levy *et al*, 1981; Van Realte *et al*, 1979):

1. ***Lower Transportation Costs***. Extensions of rural-urban roads or improvements in road conditions lowered the costs in time and money that farmers pay to get their produce to market. The roads allowed more extensive use of motorized vehicles, encouraged competition among bus and trucking firms and increased the types of road use.

2. ***Significant Increases in Agricultural Production***. The largest increases in output have been observed where complementary inputs were provided, transport was competitive and the cost of transport was a high percentage of produce price.

3. ***Change in Crop Composition***. Increased access of rural households to urban markets induced farmers to change from subsistence to commercial cultivation, and allowed farmers to respond better to market opportunities. It also allowed farmers within a greater distance from market centers to plant more perishable commercial crops.

4. ***Adoption of Commercial Inputs***. More farmers were able to use new agricultural tools, machines, fertilizers, pesticides and other commercial inputs. Usually the larger and more productive farmers benefited first, but poorer farmers also obtained substantial benefits from the adoption of commercial inputs as the market for food products increased.

5. ***More Effective Agricultural Extension***. Rural areas were served more efficiently and effectively by public agencies providing support services for agricultural development. Extension, demonstration, cooperative and informational programs were usually established after roads made service delivery easier for city-based government agents.

6. ***Spread of Processing Activities***. New rural-urban physical linkages allowed agro-industrial, processing and commercial enterprises providing consumer goods to locate along road corridors as well as in towns and cities. In some places, small-scale manufacturing and processing enterprises competed with cottage industries, but they also made available to rural households a wider variety of manufactured goods at lower cost.

7. ***Increased Land Values***. The value of land along new access roads usually increased, encouraging more intensive use of land and more extensive cultivation of high-value commercial crops.

8. *New and More Effective Marketing Patterns.* The construction of rural-urban road linkages increased agricultural and related marketing activities and restructured local marketing patterns. Periodic markets were often consolidated or displaced by daily markets; the farmers closest to roads and market centers could by-pass middlemen and obtain a higher return for their products; informal sector or small-scale marketing activities increased along roadsides, providing new income-earning opportunities especially for women and children.

9. *Increased Access to Off-Farm Employment.* New roads allowed larger numbers of rural households to obtain income from off-farm employment opportunities in towns and cities by shortening commuting distances and lowering transportation costs.

10. *Easier Access to Social and Public Services.* The creation of stronger physical linkages between rural and urban areas has also increased the intensity with which rural families use social services, recreational facilities, health clinics and some types of educational facilities in towns and cities to which they had no previous access.

CONCLUSIONS

Governments can do much to strengthen the ability of towns and cities to perform economic and social functions that support and stimulate agricultural development by locating investments in services, facilities, infrastructure and productive activities in places where the rural population will have the most access to them, or by investing in projects that will increase the access of the rural population to towns and cities performing those functions. But investing in production facilities, infrastructure and support services in towns and cities, or linking them more effectively to their rural hinterlands, is only one of many actions that must be taken in rural regions to expand agricultural productivity and raise the income of rural households. Strengthening linkages between rural areas and cities by constructing or improving access roads, for example, can have the kinds of beneficial effects described earlier only if it is a part of a more extensive program to support agricultural development and raise the income of rural households. Evaluators of farm-to-market road projects point out that "only if combined with rising agricultural incomes and policies that supported small-scale commercial and industrial enterprises could rural road construction assist the growth of commerce and production benefiting poor people." They concluded that "to provide farmers with improved access to markets, more than rural road construction was usually necessary. Also needed were a marketing system that could handle increased production, price incentives, complementary services and inputs, and a transport industry that could respond with more and better services at lower prices" (Anderson and Vandervoort, 1982, pp. 16-17).

Strengthening the functions of urban centers must be done carefully, incrementally and strategically in most developing countries. Not all towns and cities in a region can or should have a full range of services, facilities and infrastructure. One of the benefits of having a well developed and integrated system of towns and cities is that it provides access to a wide range of functions for a large number of people without each settlement having to provide all of them.

Thus, one of the major tasks of regional planning is to ensure that investments in services, facilities, infrastructure and productive activities are located strategically in towns and cities that can serve a wide area, and that linkages are forged between these and other settlements in a region so that more people have access to them. Regional planning can provide the information needed to help planners and policy-makers make investment and location decisions that will achieve these goals (Rondinelli, 1985).

REFERENCES

Abbott, J.C. "The Development of Marketing Institutions." In *Agricultural Development and Economic Growth*, edited by H.M. Southworth and B.F. Johnston. Ithaca: Cornell University Press, 1967.

Anderson, G.W., and Vandervoort, C.G. *Rural Roads Evaluation Summary Report*. Program Evaluation Report No. 5. Washington: US Agency for International Development, 1982.

Bromley, R. "Markets in Developing Countries: A Review." *Geography*. Vol. LVI Part 2 (1971):124-132.

-------. "Market Centres, Marketing Policies and Agricultural Development." *Regional Development Dialogue*. Vol. 5, No. 1 (1984): 149-165.

Cobb, R., Hunt, R., Vandervoort, C., Bledsoe, C., and McClusky, R. *Liberia: Rural Roads*, Project Impact Evacuation No. 6. Washington: US Agency for International Development, 1980.

Gibb, A. Jr. "Tertiary Urbanization: The Agricultural Market Centre as a Consumption Related Phenomenon." *Regional Development Dialogue*. Vol. 5 No. 1 (1984): 110-141.

Hapgood, D. and Millikan, F. *Policies for Promoting Agricultural Development*. Cambridge, Mass: Center for International Studies, Massachusetts Institute of Technology, 1965.

Johnston, B.F., and Kilby, P. *Agriculture and Structural Transformation*. New York: Oxford University Press, 1975.

Lam, T. "Food for the City: The Role of the Informal Sector." *GeoJournal* Supplemental Issue 4 (1982): 49-59.

Lele, U. *Food Grain Marketing in India: Private Performance and Public Policy*. Ithaca: Cornell University Press, 1971.

Levy, I., Zuvekas, C. Jr., and Stevens, C. *Philippines: Rural Roads I and II*, Project Impact Evaluation No. 18. Washington: US Agency for International Development, 1981.

Mellor, J.W. "Toward a Theory of Agricultural Development." In *Agricultural Development and Economic Growth*, edited by H.M. Southworth and B.F. Johnston. Ithaca: Cornell University Press, 1967.

Mittendorf, H.J. "Useful Strategies for Developing Countries Striving to Improve Food Marketing Systems." In *Rural Change*, edited by G. Johnson and A. Marender. Totowa, NJ: Allenheld and Osmun, 1981.

Mosher, A.T. *Getting Agriculture Moving: Essentials for Development and Modernization*. New York: Praeger, 1966.

Rondinelli, D.A. *Applied Methods of Regional Analysis*. Boulder, Co: Westview Press, 1985.

--------. "Cities and Agricultural Development: The Urban-Rural Connection." *Regional Development Dialogue* Vol. 5 (1984):1-18.

--------. *Secondary Cities in Developing Countries: Policies for Diffusing Innovation*. Beverly Hills, CA: Sage Publications, 1983.

--------. "Towns and Small Cities in Developing Countries." *Geographical Review* Vol. 73 No. 4 (1983a): 379-395.

Rondinelli, D.A., and Ruddle, K. *Urbanization and Rural Development: A Spatial Policy for Equitable Growth*. New York: Praeger Publishers, 1977.

Van Realte, G.R., Singer, S., Severn, B., and Colon, J.C. *Colombia: Small Farmer Market Access*, Project Impact Evaluation Report No. 1. Washington: US Agency for International Development, 1979.

Wharton, C.R. "Editor's Introduction: The Execution of Agricultural Development," In *Subsistence Agriculture and Economic Development*, edited by C.R. Wharton. Chicago: Aldine Publishing Co. 1969.

Weitz, R., Pelley, D., and Applebaum, L. *New Settlements and Employment*. Rehovot: Settlement Study Centre, 1976.

URBAN/URBAN RELATIONS AND RURAL REGIONAL DEVELOPMENT

Michael L. McNulty

URBAN GROWTH AND RURAL DEVELOPMENT

Regional and national growth inevitably result in the emergence of urban centers of production, distribution, consumption, service and administration. The relationships between these centers change according to the development context and to the period in growth of the region or the nation, and are both spatial and functional. The spatial aspects refers to the number and relative location of such centers, and the functional - to the economic, social, political and other linkages which exist between the centers. The nature of the relationship between the spatial and functional attributes of urban systems has been studied extensively by geographers and regional scientists.

This paper discusses the nature of that relationship in developing rural regions of the Third World. It is argued that the experience of colonialization in many countries of the Third World adversely affected the development of a strong national system of urban centers, and that this in turn has slowed the pace of rural development and frustrated the growth of viable regional economies. It is further suggested that the actions of national governments and international donor agencies since independence have exacerbated the problem. Policies of national governments and projects of donor agencies have failed to provide for the essential intra- and inter-urban infrastructure required to facilitate rural production. Strengthening urban/urban and rural/urban linkages through the provision of physical and human infrastructure is considered an important concomitant, if not a prerequisite, to rural development. Rural development projects which do not recognize this will continue to fail.

Urban centers emerge to serve specific economic, social and political purposes. As such, cities are a reflection of the organizing principles of the economy, society and policies they serve. Analysis of the spatial pattern of urban growth in a region cannot meaningfully be undertaken without an appreciation of the functional relationships which maintain that pattern, the organizing principles which are its reason for existence, and the institutions which are the means for implementing those principles. The following observations are intended to facilitate the discussion of these aspects of urban/urban relations as they emerge in the course of regional development. Although the time-honored principles of Central Place Theory are often invoked to describe - if not explain - the nature of urban/urban relationships, the comments below derive less from that source than from the author's interpretation of the nature of inter-urban relations as observed in countries of the Third World. A further *caveat*, these observations rely rather too heavily on the experience of urbanization in Africa, particularly West Africa.

MAJOR ATTRIBUTES OF URBAN SYSTEMS IN LDC

Wherever centers existed prior to European colonization, they tended to be semi-autonomous centers of political and economic systems relatively limited in their geographic scope. But the emergence of important centers of commerce and administration was interrupted by the imposition of colonial rule. The 'spatial order' which existed to serve indigenous political and economic interests was disrupted, and replaced by a new, colonial spatial order.

For example, the settlement system of West Africa prior to colonial penetration consisted for the most part of small dispersed settlements based on local economies of agriculture and rural production. Although trade existed both locally and over long distances, there was no highly developed urban system nor a well articulated marketing structure. In the early stages of regional development, it is not uncommon to find small dispersed autonomous regional economies with relatively little long-distance trading between and among them. Such rural settlements are frequently self-sufficient and maintain their semi-autonomous economic structures.

The classical model of regional development would suggest that small dispersed settlements begin to change as *functional specialization* creates opportunities for gaining economies of scale. Individual members of the community and particular settlements begin to specialize in the production of one or another commodity or service. Such functional specialization among individuals and among sub-communities within the rural settlements also lead to an *area specialization*. Now specific locations within the region begin to take on characteristics of more specialized production areas. As functional and area specialization begin to take place, there is a need for greater interaction among the now functionally specialized settlements. As a consequence, demand for transportation and other commercial activities associated with the marketing and exchange of goods begins to increase, and centers of production, distribution and consumption which are associated with the regional development process emerge. In a fully integrated exchange economy, the developing settlement systems are frequently characterized by hierarchical structures in which major centers dominate the flow of economic and other interactions; secondary cities play more localized roles as sub-centers for the distribution and collection of goods; and the lower level of market towns and service centers serves the immediate needs of the rural population.

This ideal sequence, which has been described in a number of conceptual works (Johnson, 1970; Friedman, 1973) and has served as a basis for much of the planning literature on rural development in Third World countries (Rondinelli, 1978; UNESCAP, 1979), failed to develop in much of the Third World. The so-called 'spatial order' of the developing countries was affected dramatically by the imposition of colonial rule. Colonial rule did not promote regional specialization and exchange of goods within the national economy. On the contrary, it integrated rural economies directly into the colonial economy, which transcended the regional and even the national territory and linked production areas into a global system of economic production and exchange. Specialization thus took place on a scale far greater than that which might have occurred within the national economy.

The resulting economies have been characterized by one author as 'warped' (Buchannon, 1964). The urban system which emerged to serve this colonial economic order was similarly distorted. Instead of a well organized and articulate system of settlements serving national and local interests through reciprocal economic exchanges, a rather simplistic structure emerged the characteristics of which have been linked to that of a dendritic system of physical drainage patterns. Major centers were located along the coast, while secondary and tertiary centers gathered along transportation routes that spread leaf-like into the interior and provided the basis for the extraction of economic wealth. These colonial systems have been described as having several features which distinguish them from settlement systems designed to serve national interests (McNulty, 1970).

It may be argued that the settlement systems which developed under colonial rule have ill-served national development and, as a consequence, they continue to be a major source of problems for regional development even after independence. The task in many developing countries is to re-orient and to de-colonize the urban systems so as to serve better the national goals and objectives. This means that an increasing number and variety of functions have to be performed at existing centers and at new centers developed to facilitate inter-regional and, thereby, national economic exchange. This process would lead to a greater complexity of urban systems and to a higher degree of 'coherence' in which intra- and inter-urban interdependence increases and functional complexity gives rise to spatial complexity in the urban system. The emerging urban system is both functionally and spatially integrated to serve national economic goals.

But few of the newly independent countries have undertaken the requisite investments in physical and institutional infrastructure to effectively change the nature of urban systems. Urban policies in many African countries, for example, have demonstrated an ambivalence to the role that cities are expected to play in national development. In the past three decades, Africa has witnessed major changes in the approach to urbanization by governments, policy makers, international donor agencies and academics. These changes have given rise to often contradictory policies with respect to urban development, and programs funded by international donor agencies have reflected a similar ambivalence. In the three decades that passed since most African countries became independent, major changes have been observed in the role ascribed to urbanization. In the 1960s cities were expected to play a major part in the emergence of national economies; they were conceived as focal points for industrial development and served as international show cases for the newly independent governments. In the 1970s cities were viewed as a drain on national development and were held responsible for the decline of the rural economy, as urban-based political and economic elites consumed a disproportionate share of the national resources. In the 1980's a new approach is emerging concerning the nature of the symbiotic relationship between urban and rural development.

The ambivalence of governments and international donor agencies, with regard to the proper role of urban investments in national development frustrated the emergence of a well integrated and viable national urban system. The single-minded focus on urban-industrial growth in the period immediately following independence and the emphasis on rural-agriculture which followed in many governments were equally misplaced. Each has contributed to policies and development projects which failed to understand the essential nature of the relationship between urban settlements, and misinterpreted the role of the relationship between urban growth and rural development in promoting national growth.

In the decades following independence, a combination of national government policies and projects of international donor agencies frustrated the emergence of strong rural-urban linkages, interregional trade and development. National government policies were often motivated by the fear of strengthening regional, political and economic interests that might challenge the capital, and thereby neglected the growth of secondary cities and market towns. International donor agencies which were pursuing lending policies based more on prevailing theoretical and polemical considerations than on an understanding of African regional development, first overemphasized the importance of the largest urban centers and later abandoned them for a myopic focus on rural development. The result was that the essential infrastructure, both physical and institutional, was ignored.

In recent years, the 'urban anathema' ethic that has pervaded development theory and donor agency progamming since Michael Lipton (1977), and before, has thwarted the process of a 'naturally' emerging set of secondary towns and market centers, and actually *reinforced* the dominance of the larger cities. The rural strategy which has dominated recent thinking on development has exacerbated the problem by couching any investments in urban infrastructure, services, management and planning in pejorative terms - urban bias, exploitative, parasitic etc. Lack of investment, inadequate revenue generation and poor management capability have crippled many otherwise healthy regional service centers. The costs of this inefficiency are borne by rural and urban residents alike, and each would share in the benefits which might accrue from an improvement in these conditions.

But what promotes the emergence of a well integrated, mutually reinforcing system of settlements? It is argued that such developments will not take place unless there is a decentralization of political and economic power and responsibility which gives rise to reciprocal development. A further requirement is increased investments in urban and inter-urban infrastructure to facilitate commercial and other development in regional centers (Rondinelli, 1983). Investment in infrastructure involves not only physical infrastructure, but also human and administrative infrastructure. There is a need to increase the administrative, planning and management capabilities of secondary centers and regional towns so that they can promote and facilitate development in their surrounding regions.

It is essential that the linkages between rural and urban centers be improved through judicious investments in infrastructure, and that local development be promoted through an extension of these linkages. The argument that has been presented so far suggests, that there are essential linkages between urban centers and between urban and rural areas which have been largely neglected both by national policy-makers and by international donor agencies in their preparation of development projects. What, then, are some of the essential linkages that are required to promote urban and rural development?

URBAN/URBAN AND RURAL/URBAN LINKAGES

Although frequently used, the term 'linkages' refers to a multitude of formal and informal flows of goods, services, messages, capital and people between urban areas. Among the many flows that can be characterized as linking the urban and rural systems are the following.

MIGRATION

The movement of people within urban areas and between rural and urban areas involves long-term and short-term flows of both a permanent and a temporary nature. Such moves encompass the circular movement of people between rural and urban labor markets, as well as the voluntary and involuntary movements of people from rural areas to urban environments in search of greater opportunities or escape from deteriorating rural economic and environmental conditions.

CAPITAL FLOWS

Capital flow involves the transmission of capital between urban and rural areas through informal and formal channels, i.e. remittances, postal orders, bank transfers, etc.

GOODS

Essential inputs to agricultural and non-farm production, as well as many consumer products, flow among urban centers and between urban and rural areas. This flow of goods also involves the evacuation of both agricultural products and products of non-farm employment.

SERVICES

A number of essential services, to both production and people, provide important linkages between service providers and their urban and rural clients. The lack of essential services for production and the inaccessibility of many human services have been the subject of much research, and the deleterious impact of their absence has been noted by many researchers (Rushton, 1986).

ADMINISTRATIVE LINKAGES

This involves the formal and informal links between individuals and institutions within urban and rural settings. Institutional linkages are essential for the flow of goods, services, capital and people between various sectors of the economy, and for their smooth functioning.

It is possible to direct rural-urban relations towards a functional complementarity that can be mutually developmental. The new relations between urban centers can be characterized by reciprocity, inter-urban exchange and functional inter-dependence reflecting regional specialization in mutual reinforcing patterns of urban growth. Analysis of existing urban/urban relations should seek to identify the major linkages that define the nature of the political, economic and social orders served by those cities. Obstacles of a policy, political or fiscal nature, which inhibit the development of secondary and local centers of production and services, should be identified and removed.

CONCLUSIONS

In the decades ahead developing countries will have to undertake the rebuilding of infrastructure, both intra-urban and inter-urban. Such infrastructure is essential to promote the emergence of a national economy, linked through a system of interregional trade and taking advantage of interregional complementarities.

Promotion of the regional and national development in the decades ahead will entail an increased emphasis on both physical and institutional infrastructure. But first, there must be a political ambition to pursue genuine national development - including the promotion of regional growth and decentralization of administrative authority. Are the governments of the Third World willing to run the risk of greater regional autonomy in order to promote national development? Are international donor agencies willing to fund projects that do not conform exactly to the prescriptions of their current agricultural emphasis? Are researchers prepared to engage in the type of empirical research so urgently required to understand the nature of the rural-urban dynamics in developing countries?

REFERENCES

Baskin, C.W. *Christaller's Central Places in Southern Germany*. Englewood Cliffs: Prentice Hall, 1966.

Buchannon, K. "Profiles of the Third World." *Pacific Viewpoint* Vol. 5 (1964):97-126.

Friedmann, J. *Urbanization, Planning and National Development*. Beverly Hills: Sage, 1973.

Johnson, E.A.J. *The Organization of Space in Developing Countries.* Cambridge, Mass.: Harvard University Press, 1970.

Lipton, M. *Why Poor People Stay Poor: A Study of Urban Bias in Rural Development.* London: Temple Smith, 1977.

McNulty, M.L. "West African Urbanization." In *Urbanization and Counter-Urbanization*, edited by B.J.L. Barry. Beverly Hills: Sage, 1976.

Rondinelli, D.A., and Ruddle, K. *Urbanization and Rural Development: A Spatial Policy for Equitable Growth.* New York: Praeger, 1978.

Rushton, G. "Use of Location-Allocation Models for Improving Geographical Accessibility of Rural Services in Development Countries." *International Regional Science Review*, Vol. 9 No. 3 (1986):217-240.

UNESCAP. *Guidelines for Rural Centre Planning.* New York, 1979.

RURAL/URBAN DYNAMICS IN REGIONAL PLANNING: EXAMPLES FROM UNDERDEVELOPED REGIONS

Gerald J. Karaska and Eric S. Belsky

This paper reports on attempts to incorporate spatial concepts and models into the development plans of Third World countries. As part of a research program for the United States Agency for International Development (USAID), American geographers and regional scientists have served as advisors to the governments of numerous Third World countries that have expressed a desire to pursue development plans which focus upon regional planning. For all cases, the interest in regional planning was expressed as a need to decentralize investments and authority so that growth could be promoted in areas outside the core region.

This approach to regional planning is based upon the fundamental assumption that widespread development is coincident with investments in a geographically dispersed pattern (Bromley, 1983; Friedmann, 1966; Kuklinki, 1981; Mabogunje, 1980; Renaud, 1981; Rondinelli and Ruddle, 1978). The concentration of investments in one or a few large cities will not automatically result in the spread of development through trickle-down processes; the spread effects of investments as in most countries are highly constrained. At the same time, many of the services, facilities and productive activities that are needed for regional development cannot be provided economically or efficiently to widely dispersed populations living at very low densities. Few developing countries have sufficient financial resources to simultaneously offer a wide range of basic services everywhere. Essential services and facilities must be located in places that have a sufficiently large concentration of population or a broad enough market area to support them economically. Thus, if economic development is to be achieved with greater social and geographical equity, investments must be made in a pattern of 'decentralized concentration.' That is, investments must be strategically located in settlements that can serve a large population living in and around them, and to which people living at relatively low densities in rural areas have easy access.

This pattern of 'decentralized concentration' can be achieved most efficiently and effectively through an *articulated and integrated system* of settlements (Johnson, 1970; Rondinelli and Ruddle, 1978). A hierarchical or diffuse settlement system can provide both the critical mass of services and facilities needed in rural areas to increase agricultural productivity and income, as well as provide the trade, transportation, administrative and social linkages that integrate a region into a self-sustaining economy.

In 1978, USAID initiated a program to investigate the feasibility of incorporating spatial planning into the development plans of a few Third World countries. This program - called the *Urban Functions in Rural Development Project* (UFRD) - was formulated as an alternative to the then dominant rural development strategy, 'Integrated Rural Development (IRD),' which repeatedly ended in failure and abandonment (Belsky and Karaska, 1984a; Rondinelli and Ruddle, 1978). The Integrated Rural Development approach was a strategy of development for small rural regions, in which large investments in infrastructure were made in such a way that the effects of one project or investment could be incorporated into another project. This 'comprehensive' plan covered many different components of the regional economy and was designed to effect region-wide development. While the 'comprehensive' or integrated character of the plan is conceptually valid, its application invariably failed because coordination between sectoral or line agencies proved impossible (Honadle *et al.*, 1980). Even when regional planning authorities or agencies were specifically formed to deal with the complexities of coordination and integration, the task proved formidable. Thus, by the late 1970s, it became apparent to development planners that another approach to regional or area planning was needed.

URBAN FUNCTIONS IN RURAL DEVELOPMENT PROJECT

The concept of Urban Functions in Rural Development Project (UFRD) was simple, and was based on the notion that there is a symbiotic relationship between urban centers and rural areas (Hansen, 1972; Johnson, 1970). Cities were the sites of establishments the functions of which were to serve rural areas; rural areas, in turn, provided the products marketed in the towns. Since each depends upon the other, development should be planned to enhance the growth of both.

The general approach of UFRD was essentially an analysis of the settlement system in a region, which (1) identified the settlements that could most effectively act as service, production and trade centers for their own populations and that of surrounding areas; (2) determined the strength of the linkages among the settlements themselves, and between them and their rural hinterlands; and (3) delineated areas in which people have little or no access to town-based services and facilities (Rondinelli and Evans, 1983).

There were four demonstration projects of UFRD in the Philippines, Bolivia, Upper Volta and Cameroon. Appropriate methodologies were developed for each country in the context of its socioeconomic characteristics. The basic methodology common to all the demonstration projects included: (1) making an inventory of the functions found in the cities and towns in the study region; (2) measuring the degree to which those town services penetrated into rural areas; and (3) delimitating (mapping) the rural areas served by each city and town.

To briefly illustrate the character of the analysis, consider that in the Philippines case study there were: 2 provincial centers, 11 local service centers, 43 rural service centers and 1,363 small centers. The two largest centers have a wide array of functions, while the smaller towns have increasingly fewer activities. A combination of time-distance analyses, linkage analyses, analytical mapping and service area clustering enabled planners in the Bicol River Basin to broadly outline the service areas of various functions and of the major settlements, as well as the functional sub-systems of settlements within the region. This combination of analyses revealed that the Bicol River Basin was *not* an integrated economic or physical region. Independent functional sub-systems of settlements tended to cluster around the two large urban centers, each primarily serving a small network of towns and villages in the surrounding area and within its own province. Transport routes in the other provinces converged at these two cities, which were also the largest markets in the basin. Smaller market centers were usually linked to one or the other of these central cities. Most of the higher order services and facilities were concentrated in the two large centers.

The accessibility and service area studies also showed that relatively little interaction occurred between the two provincial cities: the level of market trade between the two cities was negligible; and travel volume was less than 230 person-trips per day, a low and insignificant volume for a region with 700,000 hectares of land and 1.7 million people. The service areas of major functions located within each center deteriorated rapidly with distance.

The main highway provided the most important physical linkage and means of access to services and facilities for people living outside the major towns. People living only a few kilometers off the main road often had to travel for long periods of time to get to towns and market centers. The cost of transporting goods to market for farmers who lived off the main roads was nearly six times that of farmers living along the main highway or a connecting provincial road. Marginal and peripheral areas that generally had little or no access to towns and the functions located in them, showed the highest levels of poverty.

The UFRD projects proved to be valuable exercises in describing rural-urban dynamics in the demonstration regions. As field activities, the UFRD projects served to enhance the awareness of local planners to the spatial character of the planning region (Belsky and Karaska 1984a; Bromley, 1983). However, when the time came to use this information in a decision-making, planning process concerning investments and their implementations, planners could not or did not choose to use the spatial information. It appears that the methodology was too abstract or too far removed from the day-to-day realities of sectoral agencies who, in fact, make the actual investment decisions (Belsky and Karaska, 1984a).

A MARKETING STRATEGY

Beginning in 1985, modifications were introduced into the UFRD methodology with the intention of making the conceptualization of rural-urban dynamics more operative for feasible programs. This new approach assumes a two-pronged strategy: one focuses upon the smallest towns in the region (the market towns), the other concentrates on the larger towns (the secondary cities). Further, this approach assumes a sectoral perspective, so that the *marketing* of specific agricultural products is now the focus of the small towns analysis; manufacturing and service provision are the major considerations of the larger-town analysis, as they affect employment generation and influence agricultural productivity. In this way, the research can appear more meaningful to investment decisions and rural-urban dynamics can be clearly articulated.

The settlement system in underdeveloped region essentially performs three functions, which can be described as sets of transactions (Ortiz, 1967). One set of flows describes products which originate outside the region and are distributed through the hierarchy of towns in the form of nested trading zones (Berry, 1967); these flows describe the *retail trade* activities which serve local consumption. Another set of transactions consists also of consumption relationships, but they refer to the flows of products which originate within the region. This type of transaction differs from the former set, in the case of rural households, in that the sites of the transactions are *periodic markets*. Periodic markets operate in the towns on specific days of the week, usually only one day a week (Bromley, 1971; Smith, 1979). They do not constitute a clearly distinct set of hierarchical relationships between the towns; rather, they perform functions only for limited areas around each market town.

A third type of transaction is described by flows of agricultural products originating at local farms but destined for *export* from the region. This production/trade/export activity generates income for local traders and producers, which, in turn, drives the consumption function (Hanssen-Bauer, 1982). In effect, this set of marketing transactions describes the 'lead' sector that initiates the economic impulses which drive the rural agricultural economy. As a development strategy, intervention in this chain of marketing transactions could be an effective way of stimulating growth.

Studies of this regional marketing system in underdeveloped regions have revealed its unique nature and pointed to some spatial characteristics which have profound implications for planning (Hanssen-Bauer, 1982; Mintz, 1955; Ortiz, 1967). In the marketing system agricultural products move from farmgate, through the hands of several middlemen (where a product is sorted by quality and bulked into larger lots), into the possession of 'buyers' from outside the region. Some distinguishing characteristics of the system are:

1. There are many small producers;
2. There are many traders;
3. There are many levels of traders;

4. Households perform dual roles as both producers and traders;

5. Prices are individually negotiated and not determined by usual, supply/demand considerations;

6. Constant trading partners are established on the basis of credit relations evolved over time to cope with capital scarcity;

7. Personal relationships are an extremely important influence on behavior.

Following from these characteristics, our studies in Ecuador have revealed that spatial accessibility in the system is very limited because traders can deal only with a small number of producers and other traders (Karaska *et al.*, 1985). For example, (1) markets are located near a small producing region, which is also the residence of the producers and traders; (2) products traded in the market originate in the producing region and are traded within the same market or in another, nearby market; (3) traders or middlemen participate in only a few markets, and the majority of the traders (especially women) participate in only one market; and (4) products flow directly from the market to destinations outside the region, bypassing the larger towns of the region.

POLICY IMPLICATIONS

This spatial model of marketing in underdeveloped regions is meaningful only if it is useful to planners as they decide where to make appropriate interventions in the regional system. Certain objectives must therefore first be articulated, and goals might include the following: (1) farmers receive a higher and more predictable income from the sale of their crops; (2) transportation costs and operating costs to traders be lessened so that the net income of both traders and products is raised; (3) consumers in all parts of the country enjoy a more dependable, lower cost, and higher quality food supply; (4) the necessary investments in plant, machinery and labor be concentrated in enterprises designed to facilities the working of a free and open market, accessible to all participants.

Based upon our research and intensive discussions with planners in Third World countries, we have concluded that the central issue that must be resolved before any major interventions are planned for the marketing system is *whether* that system should be modified within the existing structure or undergo major structural changes. The issue is not an easy one to resolve, and there are obvious gaps in the information needed to make informed judgements. The debate over the extent to which the regional marketing system should be altered revolves around the issue of whether the properties of the system described above constitute an ineffective system that could be improved by fundamentally altering any or all of its structural characteristics.

MODIFY WITHIN THE EXISTING STRUCTURE

There are those who argue that the structure of the existing system provides for the maximum possible benefits to rural households and for the most efficient flow of products and locally produced consumer durables that can reasonably be expected, given the prevailing production patterns, economic conditions and levels of infrastructure. To support their claims, they argue that:

1. Dispersed sites constitute a decentralized system that brings employment and income generating opportunities closer to a wider number of people (producers, traders and consumers).

2. Dispersed sites maximize the accessibility of rural producers to markets and minimize weight loss and spoilage in transport as well as the amount of time that producers must devote to marketing.

3. Large numbers of traders/intermediaries allow for the many small lots of produce marketed by peasants to be bulked economically, and they provide outlets for produce that larger traders could not handle.

4. Large numbers of traders/intermediaries facilitate competition.

5. Many rural households depend upon wages from salaried work in the *feria* or profits from petty trading, which are important contributions to their total income.

6. The need to establish personal relations to achieve both creditability and to qualify for informal forms of credit help to ensure that individually negotiated prices are fair for buyers and sellers.

While these people believe that the current system should not be radically restructured, they do perceive a number of deficiencies in the system, such as: loss of weight in transport due to poor feeder roads and lack of rural mass transit; spoilage due to lack of adequate storage and poor marketing practices by intermediaries; unfair prices due to lack of fair weights and measures; less than optimal deployment of capital and returns to capital due to lack of efficiency in the operations of many intermediaries; difficulty in attracting agro-industries due to difficulty in ensuring adequate flows of produce to would-be investors; and difficulty in responding flexibly to increased flow of goods through the markets due to difficulty in foreseeing long-term increases. However, they believe that all these deficiencies can be resolved by simple interventions in the existing structure, and that it is only through slow evolutionary change that the structure should be altered.

SIGNIFICANT MODIFICATION OF THE STRUCTURE

On the other hand, there are those who perceive many of the same deficiencies of the existing structure, but believe that it is pointless to try and overcome these deficiencies within the current system. They also see additional problems with the current structure and argue that the four structural properties enumerated above are fetters on development. This group advocates all or some of the following.

1. Centralizing as much of the produce marketing in the region in one or two selected sites, well-located on main transport axes and capable of handling large volumes of trade. Decentralization is seen as contributing to waste because it prohibits economies of scale in marketing and constitutes an out-

moded and inefficient method of marketing that should be replaced by more 'modern' marketing methods, like cold storage and selling of produce at the farmgate. Centralization is conceived not only as a way of increasing economies of scale, but also as a means for attracting agro-industry, generating revenues for municipal governments and encouraging dynamic regional centers, and as a tool for regulating markets more closely to ensure fair weights, measures and prices.

2. Reducing the large number of intermediaries by replacing them with a group of highly trained and well-financed professional private or public sector firms. Large numbers of intermediaries are considered a source of waste and inefficiency in the market system, and a primary cause of large price margins between producers and consumers.

3. Strictly regulating prices in markets so that prices reflect supply and demand conditions.

Those who argue for centralizing activities, reducing intermediaries and regulating prices contend that their approach is directed at obtaining the best possible price for producers with the least amount of waste and spoilage of food resources. The opponents of this position contend that prices to producers cannot be greatly improved over what they are now to justify such an approach, that breaking from an established social marketing system can have serious and foreseen consequences on internal food distribution and exporting, that intermediaries do not contribute to a great per unit mark-up in price, and that centralizing markets will deprive many rural areas of important income-generating activities.

SUMMARY AND CONCLUSIONS

It is now clear that many Third World governments are aware that regional planning must become part of their long-term development plans. While the term 'regional planning' has a distinctive area connotation, implying that issues of decentralization and deconcentration must be addressed the interest in regions may also be interpreted to mean that coordinating development in smaller areas may be a meaningful approach. It is also encouraging to observe that spatial planning is now becoming recognized as a vital component of development plans. In that context, considerable work remains to be done to promote a better understanding of the interrelationships between actors in space, so that limited investments may have the widest and most beneficial impacts.

REFERENCES

Belsky, E. and Karaska, G. *The Urban Functions in Rural Development End of Product Assessment Report*. Worcester: Clark University/SARSA, 1984a.

--------.*A Critique of the Functional Integration Approach*. Worcester, Clark University/SARSA, 1984b.

Berry, B.J.L. *Geography of Market Centers and Retail Distribution*. New Jersey: Prentice Hall, 1967.

Bromley, R.J. "The Urban Road to Rural Development: Reflections on USAID's Urban Functions' Approach." *Environment and Planning* 15 (1983):429-432.

--------."Markets in the Developing Countries: A Review." *Geography* 56 (1971): 124-132.

Center for Policy and Development Studies, University of the Philippines, Los Banos. *Urban Functions in Rural Development: A Research in Spatial Analysis and Planning*. College, Laguna, Philippines, 1978.

Friedmann, J. *Regional Development Policy: A Case Study of Venezuela.* Cambridge: MIT Press, 1966.

Hansen, N.H. (ed.) *Growth Centers and Regional Economic Development.* New York: The Tress Press, 1972.

Hanssen-Bauer, J. *Plaza Pachano: Market Integration Intermediaries, and rural Differentiation in Tungurakha, Ecuador.* Occasional Paper No.5. Department of Social Anthropology, University of Oslo, 1982.

Honadle, G., et al. *Integrated Rural Development: Making it Work*? Washington: US Agency for International Development, 1980.

Johnson, E.A.J. *The Organization of Space in Developing Countries.* Cambridge: Harvard University Press, 1970.

Karaska, G., et al. *Project Summary Report: Rural-Urban Dynamics in Ecuador, Agricultural Marketing in the Ambato Region.* Worcester: Clark University/SARSA, 1985.

Kuklinski, A. (ed.). *Polarized Development and Regional Policies.* The Hague: Mouton, 1981.

Mabogunje, A.L. *The Development Process: A Spatial Perspective* London: Hutchinson, 1980.

Mintz, S. "The Jamaica Internal Marketing Pattern: Some Notes and Hypothesis." *Social and Economic Studies* 4 (1955): 95-103.

Ortiz, S. "Colombian Rural Market Organization: An Explanatory Model." *MAN* 2 (1967):393-414.

Renaud, B. *National Urbanization Policy in Developing Countries.* London: Oxford University Press, 1981.

Rondinelli, D.A. "Spatial Analysis for Regional Development: A Case Study in the Bicol River Basin of the Philippines." *Resource Systems Theory and Methodology* No. 2. Nagoya: The United Nations University, 1980.

Rondinelli, D.A., and Evens, H.E. "Integrated Regional Development Planning: Linking Urban Centers and Rural Areas in Bolivia." *World Development* 11 (1983): 31-53.

Rondinelli, D.A., and Ruddle, K. *Urbanization and Rural Development: A Spatial Policy for Equitable Growth.* New York: Praeger, 1978.

Smith, R.H.T. "Periodic Marketplaces and Periodic Markets: Review and Prospect." *Progress in Human Geography* 3 (1979): 471-505.

SPATIAL ANALYSIS OF REGIONAL MARKETING SYSTEMS IN THE THIRD WORLD

Michael Painter*

INTRODUCTION

The pioneering work in economic geography of Christaller (1966) and Losch (1954) made social scientists aware that a relationship exists between the spatial arrangement of a regional market system and the social and economic relations that organize the system. Subsequent work by Skinner (1965/66), Smith (1976, 1977) and others has shown that the ideal central-place hierarchies described in early models have correlates in functioning market systems, so that particular kinds of social and economic relations between participants in a system have predictable spatial manifestations.

This characteristic has become the object of considerable interest among social scientists concerned with poverty and underdevelopment in countries of the Third World. Spatial analysis of market systems enables us to understand their underlying organization on a regional level, with less of the time-consuming ethnographic analysis normally associated with market studies. Furthermore, the relationship that exists between a market system's spatial arrangement and the social and economic relationships that compose it suggests that the economic opportunities of people living within the region can be improved by modifying the location of

*The author thanks Jane Collins and participants in the Rural/Urban Dynamics seminar for comments on an earlier draft of this paper. The views expressed are those of the author and do not necessarily reflect official positions of the Institute for Development Anthropology, Clark University, or the U.S. Agency for International Development.

transport services, bulking facilities and market centers. This makes spatial analysis attractive to government and development agency planners, who may be reluctant to support regional development efforts because they associate them with high costs in money and time, and with benefits that do not appear sufficiently tangible; and who are enjoined to treat development as a technical problem rather than a political one involving competition for resources among different interest groups. The construction or improvement of physical market facilities offers a tangible product at the end of a project, and it may appear to avoid the need for explicit decisions about 'whose ox is to be gored' in a particular setting.

Karaska and Belsky's article in this volume provides an illustration for the application of spatial analysis in Ecuador. They suggest a number of ways in which changes in the spatial arrangement of the Ambato regional market system might improve the economic opportunities of the population that lives there. However, because spatial analysis is a promising analytical tool for research and planning, its limitations should also be carefully examined. Otherwise, there is a danger that, like many other useful tools, it will become saddled with a reputation for failure that arises from inappropriate application or unrealistic expectations, and will be discarded out of hand.

ORGANIZATION OF MARKETS AND MARKETPLACES

Smith (1977) has pointed out that the fruitful application of spatial analysis to the study of regional market systems is based upon an understanding of the relationship between market organization and marketplace organization. The former refers to the way in which supply and demand interact in a particular social and historical context to price commodities and the means of their production, while the latter refers to how physical channels of market exchange are organized on the ground. The application of spatial analysis to problems of regional marketing is based upon the premise that marketplace organization varies as market organization varies.

The options that are available to the participants in a market system are a function of the social relations between the exchanging parties. Relevant aspects of these social relations for shaping economic opportunity may include differences in the scale of operation or wealth between the exchanging parties, differences in the relative scarcity or socially-determined need for the goods controlled by each, or the ability of one party to outwait or outexchange the other (Smith 1977).

These kinds of relationships are, in turn, a function of the distribution of the means of production necessary to produce the commodities being exchanged in the market system. Thus, it is the prior distribution of productive resources that shapes the prices of the commodities that are being exchanged in a particular market system. While commodity prices may feed back into the costs of productive resources, over the long term commodity prices are more reflective of the distribution of resources than they are causative. The result is that those who enter into unfavorable market relations are rarely able to improve their position simply by being more productive. The smaller resource base of the disadvantaged party is depleted, while the party with greater access to productive resources accumulates capital.

Drawing upon the work of Christaller (1966) and Losch (1954), Skinner (1964/65) and Smith (1976, 1977) have shown that the kinds of social relations described above, which are associated with different patterns of market organization, have their analogues in the spatial arrangement of market systems. The earlier works hypothesized a relationship between market organization and the spatial arrangement of the marketplace. They deduced the nature of the spatial arrangement of a market under ideal conditions; located on a featureless plain and characterized by total dedication to profit maximization by all suppliers of goods, complete rationality in the selection of market centers by consumers, a differentiated and regionally integrated market economy, equal purchasing power by all exchanging parties, and unrestricted perfect competition among all parties. However, because such conditions rarely characterize the organization of real marketplaces in functioning market systems, the applications of the insights of Christaller and Losch were limited.

Skinner and Smith, however, demonstrated that functioning market systems also have characteristic spatial arrangements which act as signatures of the social relations that organize them. They defined several types of regional market systems, based upon the amount of hierarchy and differentiation among centers, and described them in terms of the social relations that one would expect to organize each type based upon the spatial arrangement. Smith (1977) defined four types of regional market systems for western Guatemala, which she argued had organizational features in common with market systems with similar spatial arrangements in other areas of the world.

The first type described by Smith was an interlocking market system, which most closely resembled the ideal central place hierarchies described by Christaller and Losch from all the systems she studied. Smith's interlocking system is characterized by a well-developed hierarchy of market centers, which contains three levels relating to one another at a 1.3.12 ratio. The features of market organization observed to accompany this spatial arrangement included a lack of political control over the rural economy, so that the interaction of supply and demand was the primary mechanism for establishing commodity prices; and a lack of concentration and monopoly in both the production and distribution of commodities. In addition, production and marketing took place in a context of growing domestic demand for the commodities produced by smallholders, and there was sufficient differentiation of production within the market region itself that most rural demand was satisfied by rural production.

The second system described by Smith was a dendritic market system, characterized by only two levels of differentiation among market centers, with a high proportion of small centers in relation to the number of large ones. Because the small centers had only weak links to one another, the prices for commodities not in demand by the larger centers were determined according to local conditions only. Only commodities which were imported to the region through the larger centers or local products which they collected and redistributed were priced on a regional level. Smith found that the dendritic system is characterized by monopoly control of market centers and transport facilities by traders from outside the region. As a result the participation of smallholders in commerce was low. Most commodities which left the local areas where they were produced were transported out of the region altogether, and local areas were heavily dependent upon commodities imported from outside the region. While the dendritic system was 'efficient' from the point of view of exporting goods from the region or distributing goods imported to the region from elsewhere, it offered few opportunities for greater local participation in commerce, or for regional economic growth and development.

The third type of spatial arrangement described by Smith was a primate market system, where she observed a single major center with no intermediate centers and many small ones. In the primate system, local trade was monopolized by urban merchants and outsiders to the exclusion of rural smallholders, and most productive resources were held by enterprises with interests outside the regional economy. As a result of this control of commerce and productive resources by outside interests, the primate system is dependent upon less developed regions for food and labor, and upon distant and more developed economies for markets.

Finally, Smith identified what she called a top-heavy market system, characterized by a proliferation of higher level market centers and the domination of commerce by rural traders. Rural producers depended upon nearby, less developed market systems to provide many of the commodities they purchase. Production occurred in the context of declining demand for the goods and services produced in the system. This, in turn, fostered intense competition among producers and traders to the exclusion of small competitors, leading to concentration and monopoly of commercialization facilities and productive resources.

APPLICATIONS OF SPATIAL ANALYSIS

Smith and others (Smith, ed. 1976) who have applied spatial analysis to the study of regional market systems have shown that it can be a powerful diagnostic tool, capable of indicating regional inequities in resource distribution, patterns of social differentiation among the members of a regional population, and the location and distribution of productive resources in both geographic and social class terms. The ability to analyze regions in spatial terms has important implications for social science research, because it allows us to perceive clearly how the processes of development and underdevelopment define and transform empirically observable economic activities. Spatial analysis also offers the possibility of improving the quality of development planning and evaluation by making it easier to predict and identify the factors limiting economic opportunity in a region.

At the same time, it is essential to remember that, while the spatial organization of a regional market system is predictive of the social relations that organize the system, it is not causal. Spatial arrangements reflect the prior distribution of resources in the region. This distribution, in turn, reflects the production goals of those who exercise political control. The outcome of political structure over control of productive resources determines the social and economic relations that organize a market system, and hence its spatial arrangement, over the long term. Spatial analysis of a region can, therefore, be used to understand how a market system functions and why economic opportunities, or their absence, are structured the way they are by making informed hypotheses about the ways in which productive resources are distributed and controlled. By using spatial analysis in this way, one is working backward from empirical data in order to understand the underlying relationships that cause those data to be ordered in a particular way.

This does not mean that spatial analysis can only be used as an academic tool. We have a number of examples how changes in the spatial arrangement of marketplaces have improved conditions for the population of affected regions. Appleby (1976, 1978), for example, has described successful efforts by peasant communities in Puno, Peru, to establish rural markets in order to break the oligopsonistic control of urban merchants over the marketing of agricultural production.(1) It is important to remember, however, that such changes did not occur in a vacuum, but were part of a pattern of social and economic changes in the larger economy.

The establishment of rural markets in Puno in the mid-20th century provided a structure for the social relations that organized the regional food market that was an alternative for the patron/client relations that had formerly prevailed. The increased competition among merchants and the hierarchical organization of bulking and transport facilities that resulted from the establishment of rural markets provided new opportunities for peasants to participate in the market system, and the revenues they earned through the sale of food products increased. However, the success of the change in the spatial organization of the market system produced conditions that were characteristic to that particular period. Attempts to establish rural markets at the beginning of the 20th century, prior to the rapid growth in urban population, would have failed because there was no pressure on merchants to seek out new sources of supply.(2)

By the 1960s, the effects of national economic policies which were designed to keep food prices for urban consumers at a low level, but discouraged domestic food production by smallholders through measures that included the subsidized importation of food staples and the promotion of industrial cash crops for export, were becoming evident (Alvarez, 1980, 1983; Caballero, 1984; Painter, 1984b). rural producers were outcompeted in regional markets by imported food products, and demand for peasant food production was on the decline. By 1980, the market network for bulking peasant production and transporting it to urban centers was not functioning in some areas of Puno, and the major purpose of the system was the distribution of manufactured goods from the cities to the countryside (Painter, 1981 and 1986).

This example from Puno indicates that changes in the spatial organization of a market system may improve the economic opportunities it provides to those participating in it. However, the efficacy of modifying the spatial organization could not be assessed simply with reference to the spatial organization itself, but was a function of changes in patterns of resource competition. Spatial analysis could predict the nature of many of the social relationships that organized the regional market system of Puno, but not the particular economic interests and political alliances that would demand or oppose such changes. While analysis of social relationships may indicate a possibility of improving economic opportunities through the modification of spatial arrangements, the practicality and long-range sociopolitical impacts of such modifications must be a question for empirical investigation.

PREDICTIONS AND PRESCRIPTIONS

Some of the ways in which spatial arrangements are predictive of the kinds of social relations that organize a market system, and the ways in which economic opportunities will or will not be altered by changes in existing spatial arrangements,(3) are illustrated by case study material from the eastern lowlands of Bolivia and from the Peruvian case discussed above. In both cases, spatial analysis is a valuable tool for understanding how the social relations that organize the respective market systems limit the economic opportunities enjoyed by rural smallholders. However, the possibilities for improving economic opportunities through alterations in the spatial arrangements of the respective markets are quite different. Furthermore, determination of the effectiveness of spatial modifications in each case can only be made after an analysis of the social relations that underlie the distribution of the physical features of each market system.

THE EASTERN BOLIVIAN LOWLANDS

The market system of the settlement area of northeastern Santa Cruz department, in the lowlands of eastern Bolivia, resembles a primate market system (Smith, 1977) dominated by the cities of Montero and Santa Cruz. Because of their proximity to one another at the southwestern edge of the region, along the same paved road, and because they purvey essentially the same goods and services in the same rural hinterland, the two cities may be legitimately viewed as a single urban center.(4) Below this primate center, markets are small, few in number and undifferentiated in terms of the goods and services they provide.(5)

Observation of this regional market system indicates that many of Smith's deductions about the nature of social relations that organize a primate market system appear to be confirmed. First, the principal aspects of local trade are controlled by interests based outside the region. The lumber industry is dominated by sawmills that represent multinational corporations. Agents of these firms routinely disregard national laws governing the cutting and sale of trees. Logs are sawed into boards, cured and shipped to the United States or Europe for transformation into a final product that will be purchased by consumers. The major cash crops, corn and rice, are either consumed locally or transported to Montero or Santa Cruz, to firms producing livestock feed and processing rice for human consumption in other areas of the country.

Secondly, productive resources are controlled by a few large-scale enterprises with interests outside the regional economy. Settlement areas were established in areas isolated from roads, and transport facilities are controlled by a small number of companies based in Montero or Santa Cruz that are principally concerned with transporting goods out of the region. Because of their limited cash reserves and political power, smallholders are unable to compete effectively for the limited quantities of agricultural inputs available in the region, and these are consumed by large-scale commercial agricultural enterprises.

Finally, the regional economy of northeastern Santa Cruz is dependent upon less developed regional economies for labor, and on distant and more developed economies for markets. The commercial agriculture that is the principal industry in the region has developed in conjunction with the increased availability of cheap migrant labor from the highland and valley regions of Bolivia. Cotton, coffee and soybeans - which are the most important crops - are exported to Brazil, and the bulk of the region's beef production is consumed in European markets.

The unfavorable situation of smallholding settlers in northeastern Santa Cruz has its origins in unsuccessful resource competition with regional elites, whose dominance in the political and economic life of northeastern Santa Cruz was not challenged when the Bolivian government undertook the promotion of capitalist agricultural development there in the 1950s. As a result they were able to monopolize access to roads and markets, with smallholder settlement being relegated to less desirable areas. State policy promoted smallholder settlement, but took no specific action to insure access to these infrastructural facilities, or to enfranchise them politically in order that they might compete effectively for the development resources channelled into the region (Painter 1985b). On the other hand, political and economic elites from other areas of the country have, on occasion, seen fit to speak out on behalf of settler interests as a device for limiting the power of increasingly assertive regional interests of their counterparts in Santa Cruz (Painter, 1985a).

The broad outlines of the situation in northeastern Santa Cruz may be predicted by an analysis of the spatial organization of its market system. While specific details depend upon an understanding of the local context, spatial analysis is a useful tool for forming hypotheses in order to arrive at such an understanding. Moreover, since the unfavorable situation of the settlers arises from unsuccessful resource competition on a regional level, a regional plan to improve access to agroprocessing facilities, roads, transport services and markets may improve the economic opportunities available to settlers. To realize these possibilities, a program of incremental changes in the spatial arrangement of the regional market system would either need to focus on areas of economic activity not already dominated by elites, or to include specific measures to strengthen institutions representing settler interests in order to insure that they are capable of competing with entrenched interests, and that the improvements made are not simply appropriated by elites (see Painter *et al.* 1984).

PUNO, PERU

As a result of the increasing demand for food by a growing urban population and the establishment of rural market centers by the peasants, the regional market system of Puno is characterized by Appleby (1976, 1981) as an interlocking system (Smith, 1977). This characterization points to some of the potential pitfalls of spatial analysis, as it is based upon premises that have less to do with the empirical realities of production and commerce in Puno than with the difficulties of conducting region-based research. One major problem is the question of establishing regional boundaries. The Puno region, as defined by Appleby, is delimited in the east by the international border between Peru and Bolivia, and in the north by the eastern range of the Andes. In fact, the city of La Paz, Bolivia, is a major source of goods and services for rural residents in Puno, and they in turn provide it with large quantities of meat, wool and certain types of food products. Rural peasants in Puno also play an important role as intermediaries in an active commerce in manufactured goods between cities in Peru and the city of La Paz (Painter, 1981,

1984a). Likewise, selecting the eastern range of the Andes as the northern boundary for the market region of Puno has little to do with economic activity. Large numbers of peasants maintain access to lands east of the Andes, from where they market significant quantities of coffee, citrus, hardwood and gold to the Puno system (see Collins, 1981, 1984; Kuczynski-Godard, 1945; Martínez, 1969). The difficulties confronting Appleby in conducting a research project on both sides of the international border and in managing logistics on the two sides of the Andes undoubtedly left him with few practical alternatives, but the fact that he defined his boundaries in ways that bore little relationship to the flow of commodities through the region under study undoubtedly influenced his perception of its organization and functioning.

In addition, Appleby's observations compared with my own (Painter, 1981, 1986) would appear to indicate that the degree of hierarchy that one observes may be, to a large degree, a function of when one makes the observations and the location of the researcher within the system. Based in the city of Puno in the mid-1980s, Appleby observed three levels of differentiation. However, in 1980, when I conducted research from a base in the outlying province of Huancané, I was unable to find clear differentiation below primary centers. Furthermore, that part of the system concerned with bulking and transporting of rural produce to Peruvian urban centers was in advanced decay in all areas except east of the Andes. Elsewhere in the region, the system primarily served to purvey manufactured goods in the countryside. My own view of the Puno market system is that it more closely resembles a dendritic model than an interlocking one.(6)

Viewing the Puno market system as a dendritic network, one finds that many of the conditions that one would expect to find based upon the analysis of Smith are, in fact, present. There is near-monopoly control of transport facilities by traders who do not participate in commerce within the region, but are concerned with the export of products to other regions for processing and/or consumption and the transport of people travelling out of the region in search of wage-labor opportunities. These traders control access to the region's primary markets, and while there is widespread peasant participation in commerce, this operates on a small scale and is dependent upon small traders being able to buy passage on the vehicles owned by their large counterparts. The Puno region is heavily dependent upon a number of manufactured goods produced outside the region. Local artisan production has been supplanted by manufactured commodities imported from outside the region in all but a narrow range of goods of interest to tourists. Regional urban centers are heavily dependent upon processed foodstuffs imported from outside Peru at the expense of local producers. Also, because of the lack of economic opportunity in agriculture, most rural families are compelled to participate in some form of wage-labour migration out of the region in search of cash income to complement agricultural production for their own use, so that wages constitute another import upon which there is considerable dependence.

In contrast to the situation in eastern Bolivia, the limitations on economic opportunity confronting rural residents in Puno are not likely to be remedied through modifications in the spatial arrangement of the market system. The declining revenues associated with agricultural production have their origins in national agricultural policies that cannot be addressed at the regional level (Alvarez, 1980, 1983; Caballero, 1984; Painter, 1983). The same is true of the concentration of marketing and transport facilities in the hands of a small number of people (Esculies Larrabure, 1977; Figueroa, 1980). This complex of factors limits returns to rural residents to such an extent that they engage in destructive land use patterns, sacrificing long-term production and productivity in order to satisfy an immediate need to spend as much time generating off-farm revenue as possible (Collins, 1984, 1986). Because the problems facing rural smallholders in Puno are not the product of regional resource competition, but involve national decisions to favor entire sectors of the Peruvian economy over smallholder agriculture, it is very difficult to imagine how altering the spatial organization of the regional market system will have an impact on the social relations responsible for the present situation.

DISCUSSION AND CONCLUSIONS

In both the Bolivian and Peruvian cases reviewed here, spatial analysis is a powerful tool for generating hypotheses about the social relations organizing the market systems in the respective regions. The power of the approach derives from the ability of the spatial models on the one hand, to accommodate the particularities of diverse local circumstances in reference to a general theory of market organization, and on the other, to enable the researcher to be explicit about the relationship between empirically observable events, observations and behaviors and the underlying relationships that generate them. The practical implication of this is that a spatial approach can greatly simplify the process of reaching an understanding of the social and economic dynamics at work in a region for development planners and policy makers.

However, as is the case with most tools, inappropriate applications can lead to unhappy results. In the first place, the fact that something is empirically observable does not mean that it is a non-problematic unit of analysis. What one observes in a regional market system may be very much a product of how regional boundaries are defined, one's vantage point in the system, and the particular time at which observations are made. Secondly, while one can predict the kinds of factors that limit economic opportunity in a market system on the basis of spatial arrangements, there is no necessary backward linkage that will allow these factors to be addressed through changes in the spatial organization of the system. Whether or not such a linkage exists is a critical question that needs to be answered for each individual case before planning proceeds.

An important consideration in this regard is the location of the parties between whom the social relation that define market organization exist. In the case of Bolivia, the factor limiting economic opportunities for smallholding settlers is unsuccessful resource competition with regional elites. While there are linkages of various types between northeastern Santa Cruz and the national and international economies, the arena for resource competition is the region itself. In Peru, this is not the case. Smallholders in Puno are the victims of policies which are hostile to them as a class at the national level. The factors limiting their economic opportunities are the same ones that limit the economic opportunities of smallholders throughout the country in similar ways. Region-based efforts to improve opportunities are not likely to show impressive results in the absence of national policy changes designed to improve conditions for smallholders.

Deere and de Janvry (1979, page 608) have argued that unfavorable terms of trade are the most common mechanism of surplus extraction from peasants in contemporary Latin America. Insofar as the terms of trade between smallholders and the other classes participating in a regional economy can be made more favorable by improving access to productive resources through modifications in the spatial organization of market systems, the contribution of this approach promises to be great. However, the considerable insight that spatial analysis affords us needs to be employed with a critical eye in order to avoid burdening the entire approach with expectations that it cannot fulfill.

NOTES

1. Peasants received important support in this area from missionaries of the Seventh Day Adventist Church, who combined religious preaching with concern for peasant struggles for social justice in education, economic opportunity etc., as well as from radical groups in Peru and elsewhere. (See Hazen, 1974; Lewellen, 1978.)

2. See Appleby (1980) for a discussion of the relationship between urban population growth and changes in the regional economy of Puno during the 20th century.

3. Data on eastern Bolivia were gathered in 1984, as part of a research project sponsored by the Cooperative Agreement on Human Settlements and Natural Resource Systems Analysis of Clark University, the Institute for Development Anthropology, and the U.S. Agency for International Development. Peruvian data were collected in 1979-80, with support from an Inter-American Foundation Learning Fellowship for Social Change and a Fulbright-Hays Fellowship for Doctoral Research. Ethnographic information on the two cases has been presented in detail elsewhere (cf. Painter, 1981, 1984a, 1985a, 1985b, 1986; Painter *et al.* 1984; Perez, 1985a, 1985b), and will not be repeated here.

4. This does not mean that the two cities are the same. They contrast sharply in terms of their histories and the locally recognized ethnic groups that dominate political life in each. Furthermore, they resemble one another in terms of the goods and services they offer only with respect to northeastern Santa Cruz department. The hinterland of the city of Santa Cruz extends to the south and southeast, and in these areas it is not serviced by Montero (see Stearman, 1985, pp. 40-133).

5. The low level of development of the regional market system has deep historical roots in the manorial economy that controlled eastern Santa Cruz until the state began to systematically promote capitalist agricultural development with support from international donor agencies in the mid-1950s. Prior to that time, economic transactions took place in the context of patron/client relations between the owners of large estates and resident peasant populations held in place by customary obligations of personal service and debt peonage (see Heath, 1969).

6. It should be emphasized that the intent here is not to criticize Appleby, whose Puno research is without parallel in terms of scope and detail of the data collected. Rather, I wish to show how different views of the same 'empirical reality' can be a result of the circumstances under which research is conducted.

REFERENCES

Alvarez, E. *Política agraria y estancamiento de la agricultura en el Perù, 1969-1977*. Lima: Instituto de Estudios Peruanos, 1980.

--------. *Politica económica y agricultura en el Perù, 1969-1980*. Lima: Instituto de Estudios Peruanos, 1983.

Appleby, G. "The Role of Urban Food Needs in the Regional Development of Puno, Peru." In *Regional Analysis Vol.I: Economic Systems*, edited by C.A. Smith, New York: Academic Press, 1976.

--------. *Exportation and Its Aftermath: The Spatioeconomic Evolution of the Regional Marketing System in Highland Puno, Peru*. Ph.D. dissertation. Anthropology Department, Palo Alto, California: Stanford University, 1978.

--------."Markets and the Marketing System of the Southern Sierra." Paper presented to the *Symposium on Andean Peasant Economics and Pastoralism*. Missouri State University, Columbia, Missouri, 1980.

Caballero, J.M. "Agriculture and the Peasantry under Industrialization Pressures: Lessons from the Peruvian Experience." *Latin American Research Review* 19 (1984):3-41.

Christaller, W. *Central Places in Southern Germany*. Englewood Cliffs, New Jersey: Prentice-Hall, 1966.

Collins, J.L. *Kinship and Seasonal Migration among the Aymara of Southern Peru: Human Adaptation to Energy Scarcity*. Ph.D. dissertation. Anthropology Department, University of Florida, Gainesville, Florida, 1981.

--------."The Maintenance of Peasant Coffee Production in a Peruvian Valley." *American Ethnologist* 11 (1984):413-438.

Deere, C.D. and de Janvry, A. "A Conceptual Framework for the Empirical Analysis of Peasants." *American Journal of Agricultural Economics* 61 (1979):601-611.

Esculies Larrabure, O., Correa, M.R., and González del Castillo, V. *Comercialización de alimentos*. Lima: Desco, 1977.

Figueroa, A. "Política de precios agropecuarios e ingresos rurales en el Perù." In *Realidad del campo Peruano después de la reforma agraria*, edited by Centro de Investigación y Capacitación y Editora Ital Perù. Lima: Centro de Investigación y Capacitación, 1980.

Hazen, D.C. *The Awakening of Puno: Government Policy and the Indian Problem in Southern Peru, 1900-1955*. Ph.D. dissertation. History Department, Yale University, New Haven, Connecticut, 1974.

Heath, D.B. "Land Reform and Social Revolution in the Bolivian Oriente." In *Land Reform and Social Revolution in Bolivia*, edited by D.B. Heath, C.J. Erasmus, and H.C. Beuchler. New York: Praeger Publishers, 1969.

Kuczynski-Godard, M. *Estudios médico-sociales en las minas de punu con anotaciones sobre las migraciones indígenas*. Lima, 1945.

Lewellen, T. *Peasants in Transition: The Changing Economy of the Peruvian Aymara, A General Systems Approach*. Boulder, Colorado: Westview Press, 1978.

Losch, A. *The Economics of Location*. New Haven, Connecticut: Yale University Press, 1954.

Martínez, H. *Las migraciones altiplánicas y la colonización del Tambopata*. Lima: Centro de Estudios de Población y Desarrollo, 1969.

Painter, M. *The Political Economy of Food Production: An Example from an Aymara-speaking Region of Peru*. Ph.D. dissertation. Anthropology Department, University of Florida, Gainesville, Florida, 1981.

--------. "The Political Economy of Food Production in Peru." *Studies in Comparative International Development* 19 (1983):34-52.

--------. "Changing Relations of Production and Rural Underdevelopment." *Journal of Anthropological Research* 40 (1984):271-292.

--------. "Ethnicity and Social Class Formation in the Lowlands of Eastern Bolivia." Paper presented to the *Annual Meeting of the American Ethnological Society*. Toronto, Canada, 1985a.

--------. "Unequal Exchange: The Dynamics of Settler Impoverishment and Environmental Destruction in Lowland Boliva." Paper presented to the *Workshop on Lands at Risk: Local-level Perspectives*. Institute for Development Anthropology, Binghamton, New York, 1985b.

--------. "The Value of Peasant Labour-Power in a Prolonged Transition to Capitalism." *Journal of Peasant Studies* 13(4):221-239.

Painter, M., Perez Crespo, C.A., Albornoz, M.L., Hamilton, S., and Partridge, W. *New Lands Settlement and Regional Development: The Case of San Julian, Bolivia*. Cooperative Agreement on Human Settlements and Natural Resource Systems Analysis. Binghamton, New York: Institute for Development Anthropology, 1984.

Perez Crespo, C.A. "San Julián: balance y desafios." Paper presented to the *Conference on Settlement and Settlement Policy in the Amazon*. Amazon Research and Training Project, University of Florida, the Pontificia Universidad Católica del Perù, and the Instituto Andino de Estudios de Poblacion. Lima, Peru, 1985a.

--------. "Resource Competition and Human Settlement in the San Julian project of Bolivia." *Development Anthropology Network* 3(1):3-8.

Skinner, G.W. "Marketing and Social Structure in Rural China, Parts I and II." *Journal of Asian Studies* 24 91964/65): 3-43, 195-228.

Smith, C.A. "Causes and Consequences of Central Place Types in Western Guatemala." In *Regional Analysis* Vol. I: Economic Systems, edited by C.A. Smith. New York: Academic Press, 1976.

--------. "How Marketing Systems Affect Economic Opportunity in Agrarian Societies." In *Peasant Livelihood*, edited by R. Halperin and J. Dow. New York: St. Martin's Press, 1977.

Smith, C.A. (Ed.). *Regional Analysis* Vol. I: Economic Systems, and Vol. II: Social Systems. New York: Academic Press, 1976.

Stearman, A.M. *Camba and Kolla: Migration and Development in Santa Cruz, Bolivia*. Gainesville, Florida: University Presses of Florida, 1985.

Part 3: Rural Regional Services

MEETING THE NEED FOR SERVICES IN DEVELOPING RURAL REGIONS

Gerard Rushton

INTRODUCTION

The social and economic level of development of any rural region is both defined and changed by the access of its people to certain services. If any one of the services of health, education, family planning, extension, marketing and credit is inaccessible to the population, further development, in most circumstances, is curtailed and the existing level of welfare is considered to be unacceptable. Contrary to its tone, choice of 'unacceptable' is not a statement of value so much as it is a conclusion that among all possible worlds, only those in which these basic human services are accessible to all will be the worlds in which the demographic transition, the epidemiological transition and the economic-production transition will occur. Development is defined here as the occurrence of a set of conditions that will facilitate the passing of any region through these socioeconomic transitions.

During the demographic transition a region passes from a condition of high fertility and high infant mortality to a condition of low fertility and low mortality. During the epidemiological transition a population passes from a condition in which the primary causes of death are infective and parasitic diseases, diseases of the respiratory system and nutritional deficiency to one in which the primary causes of death are due to the aging process or to misadventure: cardiovascular diseases, cancer and accidents. During the economic-production transition, per capita productivity of the different sectors of the economy increases as the factors of production, including capital, are combined in more efficient ways, regions concentrate on productive activities for which they have a comparative advantage and interregional trade arises. Without human services being available, none of these changes will take place; for development theory is now clear that regions do not develop by passing inexorably through 'stages of development', but by ensuring that at every stage of development the conditions exist that will lead, at the level of both individual and the group, to the making of decisions that are consistent with these transitions.

This chapter takes one service sector, health; briefly describes the evolving patterns of health services in developing rural regions, and then discusses a number of key issues that must be resolved in order to develop appropriate health services for such areas and to select interventions that will optimally improve health in a region with available resources. Most of the issues discussed also arise when services other than health are examined in any region, so that most conclusions can be applicable to service systems in general.

TYPICAL METHODS OF ORGANIZING HEALTH SERVICES

URBAN-ORIENTED, HOSPITAL-BASED CARE

Numerous studies have examined the expenditure patterns for health in developing countries, and have found that a disproportionate share of funds are used to provide care in the urban areas with an emphasis on use for curative, hospital-based services. This 'geographical maldistribution' of resources has been found in almost every developing country examined. Garfield and Taboada (1984, page 1139), for example, cite studies that found that in 1972 in Nicaragua "although only 25 per-cent of the population lived in the capital city, half of all doctors and more than two-thirds of the professional nurses worked there. It is estimated that at the time of the revolution 60 per cent of all human and material health resources were in Managua, and 80 percent of the rural health manpower consisted of folk healers."

Barnum and Barlow (1984, page 368), noted that: "The use of large-scale physical facilities (hospitals and clinics) to provide capital-intensive curative care for limited population subgroups has fallen into justified disrepute. It is clearly recognized that these facilities do not represent a cost-effective use of resources."

Similarly, a recent report on the Indian health system (ICSSR-ICMR, 1981, page 10) concluded: "The imported and inappropriate model of health services is top-heavy, over-centralised, heavily curative in its approach, urban and elite oriented, costly and dependency creating". Alternative organization patterns were suggested by WHO, together with manpower planning policies for staffing them (Hall and Mejia, 1978).

COMPREHENSIVE, INTEGRATED HEALTH CARE SYSTEMS

In response to these findings on the ineffectiveness of urban-based services for meeting the needs of rural populations, a number of strategies were devised to solve this problem.

Comprehensive, government-provided primary health care programs were developed that made the government the main provider of medical services in rural areas. A typical method of organization, as in India, involved the creation of an infrastructure for the delivery of health services throughout the country, consisting of primary medical centers and health sub-centers. At the same time that many governments attempt to provide free services, they also often support and maintain a second health system available to special groups, such as the armed forces or other public servants. This system exists in uneasy juxtaposition with traditional health systems (Good *et al*, 1979; Leslie, 1985), which, in many countries at least, 'have been falling increasingly into disarray' (Bose and Desai, 1983, page 4).

Mobile health programs were developed to bring either special or comprehensive health services to underserved areas. Often, these represent attempts by urban-based hospitals to reach out to the rural population with appropriate health services (Macagba, 1984). In general, mobile health programs have not been successful in bringing low-cost and continuous health care to the populations they serve. Each medical college in India, for example, was supplied by international donors with three mobile clinics, with the expectation that medical students who travelled with them would be exposed to typical rural health problems and that specialized health services, not generally available at the village level, would be provided. A spot check of the daily log of one such vehicle by this author showed that, due to a shortage of funds to purchase diesel fuel, it had not moved for six months; that its medical instruments and supplies had been transferred to a local hospital; and that villages in the vicinity had asked that it not be sent to them on account of the fact that the heavy vehicle was responsible for the destruction of many granite culverts on the rural roads over which it travelled. The Planning Commission of the Indian Government has recently recommended that a critical evaluation of the scheme throughout the country should be made since the 'mobile clinics...are stated to be unwieldy and not suited to our rural conditions' (Government of India, 1983, page 101).

'Categorial' health programs were devised to control the most serious health problems. Often organized along the lines of the successful WHO smallpox irradication program (World Health Organization, 1980), these were usually designed to attack individual epidemic diseases. (In India, for example, this involved control programs for malaria, leprosy, tuberculosis, cholera, trachoma and prevention of blindness.) These programs often use specialized manpower and facilities that report back directly to a national or regional office rather than to the existing health care system in the local area.

ISSUES AND ALTERNATIVE STRATEGIES FOR ORGANIZING HEALTH SERVICES

In developing its system of health care, each government has had to determine its response to several issues, as follows.

GOVERNMENT'S ROLE IN SERVICE PROVISION

A very basic question is the role that the government defines for itself in solving problems of access to basic services. The role chosen is usually compatible with its philosophy of its role as an instrument of development. This has varied from the government as planner and provider of all basic services to a more *laissez faire* role of facilitating the means by which private providers will emerge to meet the needs of any area or group. In between these two extremes are intermediate roles, in which governments attempt to meet needs of particular target groups or target areas where access to services is problematic. The methods of need assessment and the appropriate responses to solve problems of needs differ according to the philosophical approach adopted by the government. When governments assume the role of planner and provider of services, their approach must necessarily be to modify the previous organizational forms. In health, for example, a common case is for the government to inherit a diverse and uncoordinated health care system consisting of charitable institutions, regional administered public systems, and systems designed for specific segments of the population such as those covered by a social security scheme of uneven degree of coverage. The government will usually try to rationalize and integrate these disparate systems in an attempt to expand coverage to disadvantaged groups and areas and to eliminate duplication of services.

PROMOTION OF CATEGORICAL HEALTH PROGRAMS OR DEVELOPMENT OF COMPREHENSIVE COMMUNITY-BASED SYSTEMS

There are many who insist, often on ideological grounds as much as on grounds of proven efficiency, that all health services resources should be channelled through community-based programs, and so be used to strengthen the organizational and administrative frameworks of the community and to promote health-seeking behavior patterns. However, there are others who argue that major achievements can be made by concentrating resources on a few interventions that have proved efficient. UNICEF (1984), for example, has strongly promoted the GOBI-FF strategy for reducing infant mortality and morbidity by bringing to all areas the proven techniques of growth monitoring, oral rehydration therapy for diarrhea, breastfeeding, immunization, food supplements and family planning. The counter argument (Mosley, 1984, page 4) claims that many of the social conditions associated with high rates of infant mortality are also associated with low use rates of these 'new technologies.' These authors (Caldwell *et al.*, 1983) argue that more basic changes in social conditions are necessary, and that such changes will be associated with changes in behavior patterns that will make the need for many of the bio-medical interventions unnecessary.

Studies of patterns of incidence of diarrheal diseases, for example, have linked the prevalence of diarrhea with housing conditions and parental education (Black, 1984; Freij and Wall, 1979). Intervention to interrupt transmission by changing the habits and conditions in which people live is one approach to reducing incidence of the disease. Another approach which is known to dramatically reduce deaths related to diarrhea is the "prompt administration of rehydration solutions (Hirschorn, 1980)" cited by Black (1984, page 157). The argument is basically whether efforts should be devoted to attacking the symptoms or the underlying causes of disease and death in these populations (United Nations, 1982).

THE INTEGRATION OF HEALTH SERVICES

Many countries, like India, strive to develop integrated community-based health care, and yet maintain many categorical programs implemented by different departments. India's Sixth Plan in 1981 refers to such categorical programs under different department controls as education, water supply and sanitation, control of communicable diseases, family planning, maternal and child health care, nutrition and school health, and urged that they be "properly coordinated for optimal results". An important step in integrating health services is the training of personnel capable of working in several categorical programs at the local level.

Integration of health services is often difficult because of the different patterns of ownership of resources and schemes for their administration. Garfield and Taboada (1984) compare the organization and operation of the health services system in Nicaragua before and after the 1978 revolution there. They describe the conflicts between the national association of doctors and the government, and how government control over health resources was gradually established. Public programs for rural medicine, maternal and child health and occupational medicine have been expanded and periodic health campaigns, including public health education efforts, have been organized in many parts of the country. These include immunization, malaria prophylaxis and sanitation campaigns. The campaigns also promoted the formation of local, regional and national community health councils. With such councils in place, periodic campaigns are being replaced by permanent ongoing activities, and attempts have been made to incorporate into this system many of the volunteers who contributed so much to the success of the periodic campaigns.

In the short run it is clearly easier to plan and implement a comprehensive, community-based, health care system when the government is the sole owner and provider of health resources. Many countries, however, where ownership or resources is fragmented among many public and private organizations, have made attempts to develop integrated health care systems. Bossert and Parker (1984) have made an extensive survey of such attempts and have described the political and administrative contexts which appear to be related to the effectiveness of the systems that result.

ASSESSING GEOGRAPHIC ACCESSIBILITY TO HEALTH SERVICES

An important issue is the need to make health services geographically accessible to the population. Numerous studies have shown the per capita decline in use of urban-based services with distance from the health center (Jolly and King, 1966; Rahaman *et al.*, 1982). Typical conclusions are that rates of utilization are reduced by half for every five kilometers increase in distance that a rural person must travel to a health facility, with the rate of decline being greatest for 'primary' and 'preventive' health services - the very services that need to be used to reduce infectious and communicable diseases that are so prevalent in these areas. Belcher *et al.*, (1978) reviewed the effects of a mass immunization campaign in rural Ghana, and found that the rate of children vaccinated varied from 89.2 percent at the site to 69.8 percent less than three miles away, and none more than three miles away.

Programs that are designed to reduce nutritional deficiency in the rural poor generally vary in their success in reaching the target population. Gwatkin (1979) found a well-organized distribution of 'fair price shops' in rural areas of Kerala, while Harriss (1983) found an uneven coverage and an urban service bias in the Coimbatore district of Tamil Nadu. In their field visits to a district in India, Bose and Desai (1983, page 120) found:

> that, in most cases, existing locations are very unsuitable from the point of view of ensuring equality of access to the service for all sections of the population in the area. We carry the impression that the choice of location of both PHC's and Sub-Centres has, in most cases, been influenced by criteria which patently compromised the need of maximising accessibility to the services. With regard to Sub-Centres, their inappropriate location is often traceable to the insistence that the required land should be provided free of cost of the community.

Their findings supported policy suggestions of a recent Indian Government Committee, that 'the location and siting of health institutions should be rationalized in order to maximize their accessibility for the people' (cited in Bose and Desai, 1983, page 127).

DEGREE OF CENTRALIZATION-DECENTRALIZATION OF SERVICES

One common approach to increasing the utilization of rural health clinics has been an attempt to locate them so that they are as accessible as possible to the rural population, implying a decentralization strategy (Bennett, Eaton and Church, 1982; Moore and Revelle, 1982; Patel, 1979; Rushton, 1984). Annis (1981), however, argued on the basis of his study in Western Guatemala - that a common reason why people travel only short distances to clinics is that they are not highly motivated to use them because of the poor quality of the services offered. A recurring question is whether services provided by village-level health workers achieve significantly higher levels of coverage than similar clinic-based services. Only recently did formal studies take up this question and it does appear that population coverage increased especially among the poorer sections of the population, as well as among those who because of illness, age, or cultural practices are unable to travel beyond their home village (Berman, 1984).

Wang'ombe (1984) concluded that the use of community health workers in Western Kenya 'effectively decentralizes access to basic health, creating 96 first contact points of care where there were previously only three' (page 378). Just as important, however, is the fact that at this level of decentralization of services, health workers can be involved in health promotion activities both at the individual and communal level. Wang'ombe's study is one of very few studies that document changes in behavior before and after the implementation of a geographical decentralization of services in an area. He presents a detailed cost-benefit analysis of a scheme in Western Kenya which provided primary health care through community-based programs. His costs included both system costs and reductions in user costs from the earlier and more centralized health system, associated with reduced travel and waiting time in the new system. Consumer's gain is measured as the value of the additional utilization resulting from the lowering of access costs (page 378). Wang'ombe concluded that positive net returns accrue to the study areas from the decentralized project.

ROLE OF THE COMMUNITY

The World Health Organization has become a strong advocate of the idea that rural communities can organize themselves to evaluate health conditions in their areas and to provide a major leadership role in improving health in their regions. It is argued that sufficient case studies now exist to prove that even in poor countries where the overall level of resources available for health is very low, success in reducing mortality and morbidity can be achieved through 'community based programs' (Morley, Rohde and Williams, 1983). A joint report of WHO and UNICEF (1978), known as the *Alma Ata* declaration on primary health, discusses at length the involvement of the community in health care:

> There are many ways in which the community can participate in every stage of primary health care. It must first be involved in the assessment of the situation, the definition of the problems and the setting of priorities. Then it helps to plan primary health care activities and subsequently it cooperates fully when these activities are carried out. In addition, members of the community can contribute labour as well as financial and other resources to primary health care.
> (WHO-UNICEF, 1978, page 51, quoted in Bose and Desai, 1983, page 14).

In such conditions, it is argued, health services will be appropriate, accessible, affordable and socially acceptable.

The effort to involve the community itself as the planner and provider of health-related activities is often an expression of faith in traditional rural values, as well as an attempt to halt the process of westernizing influences that, it is often argued, is embodied in and brought by the elites of the 'medical establishment' (Bose and Desai, 1983, page 4). Involving the community is, therefore, part of an overall development strategy for self-reliant development. After all, if communities succeed in organizing and managing their own health systems, the local leaders who made this possible and the decision-making procedures used could well be used to effect other kinds of developmental changes in their communities. Considering the relationships between other aspects of social-economic development and health (Mosley, 1984), such a broadening of the role of the community may well be essential to improve the health of the community. The counter argument, however, is that if the community does not already have a history of having been involved in activities to promote its own welfare, it may be unable to rise to the tasks required in a community-based health system. Without being cynical, one can argue that the role of government in many countries has been to stifle local, grassroot leadership that, in many cases, have challenged the power and the priorities of the governing elites. In such circumstances it is unlikely that governments will expect the leadership groups that emerge to work for improved health to restrict their attention to health matters, particularly when they have been asked to consider both the biological and social factors that affect the health of their community.

Jobert (1985) has shown how the Community Health Volunteers scheme in India has so far largely failed in its goal of developing popular participation in improving rural health. India's Sixth Plan in 1981 promised that communities 'would be entitled to supervise and manage their own health programs eventually' (Government of India, 1981, page 368), thus leaving to the future eventual local control over health care resources in favor of government bureaucracy which would, in the meantime, attempt to integrate the health services offered by different government departments. A fundamental problem, found throughout the world, is the question of the accountability of community health workers to the professional health organization and to their community. Scholl (1985) describes the problem in Nicaragua, and Bose and Desai (1983) discuss the same problem in India.

THE PROFESSIONALIZATION OF HEALTH CARE

Increasing the role of the community in health care planning and health system implementation reduces the role of health professionals in controlling the system and in setting the terms of their employment. In many countries, more community involvement is not supported by health professionals, particularly physicians, who often see it as a lowering of professional standards of medical treatment (Bose and Desai, 1983, page 70; Leslie, 1985, page 923). In India, the confusing relationship between the Community Health Volunteers and the professional health care system illustrates the sensitivity of this relationship. Bose and Desai (1983, page 7) observe that the community health worker 'becomes an appendage of the existing well-entrenched clinic-oriented health infrastructure, thereby transforming him into a lay agent of a professionalized health service.' The original expectation had been that the community health volunteers would act as a bridge between the health care delivery system and the community, and would initiate health promotion activities in their community. Accordingly, they must be trained not only to administer simple medical interventions, but also in the job of creating community support for health matters.

MEDICAL EDUCATION

New organizational forms for health care often require different types of training for professional, paraprofessional and volunteer personnel who will work in the system. In many countries there exists a strong tradition of indigenous systems of medicine that have proven effective for many health problems. The task of integrating them with western (allopathic) medicine while ensuring that no biases are introduced that may threaten their survival is a difficult one (Good *et al*, 1979). Medical doctors are very often reluctant to practice in rural areas, and even when they are employed by the government, they frequently regard their assignment to a rural area as a temporary hardship post before their request for transfer to an urban center is granted. Medical education in a hospital context is not representative of the conditions typically encountered in rural medical practice. Much of the training there is in the treatment of the more complex and less common diseases, whereas the real need is to learn how to treat common diseases of a developing rural region with the equipment and with the aid of the auxiliary personnel typically available there.

DETERMINANTS OF DEMAND FOR HEALTH CARE

Basic to improving health in any area is an understanding of health-seeking behavior there. Aday and Anderson (1975) formulated a conceptual model which has been the basis for many empirical studies. In their model background factors, predisposing factors and enabling factors are shown to be related to the likelihood of a person to seek health care or to act in ways conducive to the maintenance of their health. Using this model, Friede *et al.* (1985, page 135) studied the acceptance of the free DPT immunizations (diphtheria-pertussis-tetanus) by preschool children in a poor rural area of the Philippines, and found that the likelihood of a child not to be immunized was related to 'adversity factors.' They recommended that prior to any immunization campaign, a "quantitative assessment of locale-specific 'adversity factors' that are susceptible to amelioration should be made. For instance: bring the site closer; make sure the time of day is right; check if it is harvest time" (page 139).

Joy and Payne (1975) argue for a functional classification of "the nutritionally deficient population which makes it possible to relate nutritional deficiency patterns to spatial, ecological, socio-economic and demographic characteristics of the population." They note that in India, the sampling design used by the National Nutrition Monitoring Bureau ensures that in each state the coverage represents different levels of agricultural development, villages of different size and different socio-economic groups in the population. A common method for assessing nutritional deficiency (Morley and Woodland, 1979) computes the weight of each child as a percentage of the expected weight-for-age, defined as the median weight-for-age on standard growth charts. Pacey and Payne (1985, page 125) report that in Costa Rica, monitoring of nutritional status is now a regular feature of the rural health program.

Several studies have shown that nutritional deficiency is related to occupational group as well as to low income. Mosley (1984, page 9) describes recent unpublished research in Indonesia, suggesting "that the predominant cause of malnutrition may not be poor diet, but frequent recurrent infections."

The general conclusion is that efforts to improve health in any rural area must begin with an understanding of the health-seeking behavior patterns of the population (Good *et al.*, 1979), the particular health problems of the area and the factors that influence decisions which are most conducive to the maintenance of health (Cumper, 1984).

EFFECTIVE ADMINISTRATION OF SERVICE SYSTEMS

Comparative studies of the effectiveness of health care systems in developing countries have shown that differences are often related to program administration. Although there is usually a desire to leave many important administrative decisions to the local level, the capabilities of people at this level are often poor (Annis, 1981;

Bossert and Parker, 1984, page 697). Administrative training is typically weak and often in the hands of people whose training concerned the clinical aspects of health. It should not be surprising that a medical officer might have trouble organizing and managing a team of thirty professional who are dispersed throughout a rural region. Even maintaining contact in such circumstances can be extremely difficult. Despite these difficulties, Djukanovic and Mach (1975) found, in a study of a series of case studies in different countries of the world, that "the most impressive gains have been made in countries where a strong central policy has been implemented by a decentralized executive organization" (page 101).

DEGREE OF CENTRALIZATION-DECENTRALIZATION IN HEALTH PLANNING

Some countries administer their program of health planning from the center and expect each region to implement the planning program according to priorities determined at the center. Deber (1980) describes such a centralized system in the USSR. She argues that 'overplanning' inhibits creative and adaptive responses in health care provision. This might be contrasted with the decentralized health planning system of Nicaragua, which depends on community councils and local volunteer workers for its success. A recent study by Rifkin (1985) compares health planning activities for community participation in health care programs in particular areas of three countries.

THE FINANCING OF HEALTH SERVICES

Many of the plans describing the health system of an area show that in an ideal system people would be interacting locally and have their needs met locally, with fewer cases being referred to the more-professional, curative health system. Typically, however, the sources of funds for different parts of the system are different, and each part guards its allocation of resources. Transfer of resources from one part of the system to another, where returns would be greater, is therefore often impossible in practice. The Community Health Worker scheme in India, for example, began in 1978 as a scheme financed by the central government (Leslie, 1985), but by 1979 it was decided that states would have to support half the cost. Some states dropped the scheme at that point (Bose and Desai, 1983 page 55). A controversial issue is the impact of user fees on the demand for health services. To what degree can user fees be increased without appreciably affecting utilization? Are there particular groups for whom a fee-for-service would bar the access to care? Are there new sources of finance which Third World countries can tap to pay for 'Health for All'? (Abel-Smith, 1985).

EVALUATING THE EFFICIENCY AND EFFECTIVENESS OF SERVICE SYSTEMS

DETERMINING LEVELS OF CRITICAL SERVICES

Although basic services are known to play key roles in social and economic development, our knowledge is incomplete on how each service interacts with other aspects of society to influence change. It is therefore impossible to define either minimum or optimum levels of each service in any region to effect change. Even within a service sector, cost-benefit analysis of alternative interventions has only recently begun (Corrin, 1984). Although promising, these approaches must be judged to be experimental at this time. Barnum and Barlow (1984), for example, developed a mathematical model of child mortality for a study area in Cali, Colombia. They used the model to determine the allocation of resources that would most reduce infant mortality in the area. Only realistic amounts of each resources was assumed to be available. The use of such mathematical optimization models implies a level of formal knowledge about the efficacy of service intervention programs that is usually not available. Consequently, although statistical estimation of the parameters of the model based on data derived from a representative real-world setting would have been desirable, the 221 parameters in the equations of the model were specified on the basis of survey responses of "medical and health practitioners with considerable experience in the problems of delivering health services in less developed countries" (page 377). Their results were similar to those of Berelson and Haveman (1980), who made an exploratory attempt to apply benefit-cost analysis to various realistic interventions to reduce fertility in developing countries. They discovered that the judgements of knowledgeable experts appear to be essentially the same as those made by policy makers in the field.

These judgements are often made on the basis of pilot evaluations of selected interventions or even more informal data, such as 'experience in the field.' More occasionally, carefully controlled, quasi-experimental designs allow more formal methods to be used to judge the efficacy of selected service interventions (Gwatkin, Wilcox and Wray, 1980; Pebley, 1984). The scarcity of such studies, and the fact that they are not representative of other areas, leaves organizers of service delivery systems without formal guides for making optimal allocations of resources among different service systems.

ASSESSING THE EFFECTIVENESS OF A SYSTEM

The difficulties in assessing the effectiveness of a service system have led to the current practice of measuring effectiveness in one of three ways, as follows.

> *Inputs Used.* Using the hypothesis that the more inputs are used the more services must be provided, service adequacy in a region is often measured by the quantity of inputs provided. The number of people per doctor or clinic; the number of hospital beds per thousand people; the number of health camps held. This is the most primitive method of evaluation because it contains no measure of the impact of these resources on the health of the population.

Process of Care. This method measures the services provided and other things that are related to the process of care. Number of child immunizations, number of clinic visits, number of oral rehydration salt solutions given and number of prescriptions filled are examples of direct measures of services provided. Waiting time at clinics, average distance of a person from nearest clinic, the proportion of people who use a clinic are examples of process-related measures of effectiveness. Although these too do not measure the quality and effectiveness of the system directly, we do know that these measures relate to effectiveness in a more direct manner than inputs.

Outcome Measures. Outcome measures determine the results of interventions and include, for example, the reduction in infant mortality and the reductions in death from specific diseases, such as measles or diarrheal complications. This is the least used measure of effectiveness, perhaps because the ultimate causes of death and disease are not all within the control of the health care system. The argument that is gaining ground claims that changes in the health status of the population is the real test of the effectiveness of a health care system, and that a given set of resources should be used in whatever way will most reduce morbidity and mortality.

CONCLUSIONS

The predominant pattern of change in organizing services for improving health in developing rural regions has involved a move from urban, hospital-based, curative services to smaller health units which are located so as to maximize geographical accessibility, emphasising programs of health promotion and disease prevention and relying on extensive involvement of the community. The organization of health services in many, but certainly not in all, the cases has devolved to a more local administrative level, with more resources to support the system coming from the local level either in the form of fees for services rendered or in the form of providing volunteers working under the supervision of locally representative groups. It continues to be a formidable task to maintain community control over 'Community Health Workers' while at the same time integrating them into both the modern (government supported) health-care system and the traditional health-care system.

Health is being considered as a product of both social and biological conditions, and interventions that seek to change the social conditions relating to ill-health are being increasingly recommended to supplement the categorical health programs that provide curative treatments for many diseases, the prevalence of which would be drastically diminished if the social conditions of life were to be changed. Finally, in some areas an attempt is being made to determine a priority list of health interventions as a result of cost-benefit and cost-effectiveness analyses.

REFERENCES

Abel-Smith, B. "Global Perspective on Health Service Financing." *Soc. Sci. and Med.* 21 (1985):957-963.

Aday, L.A., and Anderson, R. *Access to Health Care*. Ann Arbor, Mich.: Health Administration Press, 1985.
Annis, S. "Physical Access and Utilization of Health Services in Rural Guatemala." *Soc. Sci. and Med.* 15D (1981):515-523.
Barnum, H.N., and Barlow, R. "Modelling Resource Allocation for Child Survival." In *Child Survival: Strategies for Research*, edited by W.H. Mosley and L.C. Chen. Cambridge: Cambridge University Press, 1984.
Belcher, D.W. Nicholas, D.D., Ofosu-Amaah, S., and Wurapa, F.K. "A Mass Immunization Campaign in rural Ghana: Factors Affecting Participation." *Public Health Rep.* 93 (1978):170-176.
Bennett, V.L., Eaton, D.J., and Church, R.L. "Selecting Sites for Rural Health Workers." *Soc. Sci. and Med.* 16 (1982):63-72.
Berelson, B., and Haveman, R.H. "On Allocating Resources for Fertility Reduction in Developing Countries." *Population Studies.* 34 (1980): 227-237.
Berman, P.A. "Village Health Workers in Java, Indonesia: Coverage and Equity." *Soc. Sci. and Med.* 19 (1984):411-421.
Black, R.E. "Diarrheal Diseases and Child Morbidity and Mortality." In *Child Survival: Strategies for Research*, edited by W.H. Mosley and L.C. Chen. Cambridge: Cambridge University Press, 1984.
Bose, A., and Desai, P.B. *Studies in Social Dynamics of Primary Health Care*. Delhi: Hindustan Pub. Corp., 1983.
Bossert, T.J., and Parker, D.A. "The Political and Administrative Context of Primary Health Care in the Third World." *Soc. Sci. and Med.* 18 (1984): 693-702.
Caldwell, J.C., Reddy, P.H., and Caldwell, P. "The Social Component of Mortality Decline: An Investigation in South India Employing Alternative Methodologies." *Population Studies* 37 (1983):185-205.
Cumper, G.E. *Determinants of Health Levels in Developing Countries*. Letchworth, England: Research Studies Press Ltd., 1984.
Deber, R.B. "Planning: Lessons From the USSR." *The Policy Studies Journal* 9 (1980): 286-293.
Djukanovic, V., and Mach, E.P., eds. *Alternative Approaches to Meeting Basic Health Needs in Developing Countries*. Geneva: World Health Organization, 1975.
Freij, J., and Wall, S. "Quantity and Variation in Morbidity: THAID-Analysis of the Occurrence of Gastroenteritis Among Ethiopian Children." *Intl. Jn. of Epidemiology*. 8 (1979): 313-325.
Friede, A.M., Waternaux, C., Guyer, B., de Jesus, A., and Filipp, L.C. "An Epidemiological Assessment of Immunization Programme Participation in the Philippines." *International Journal of Epidemiology* 14 (1985): 135-141.
Garfield, R.M., and Taboada, E. "Health Services Reforms in Revolutionary Nicaragua." *Am. Jn. Public Health* 74 (1984):1138-1144.
Good, C.M., Hunter, J.M., Katz, S.H., and Katz, S.S. "The Interface of Dual Systems of Health Care in the Developing World: Toward Health Policy Initiatives in Africa." *Soc. Sci. and Med.* 13D (1979):141-154.
Government of India. *Sixth Five Year Plan 1980-85: Mid-Term Appraisal*. New Delhi: Planning Commission, 1983.
Gwatkin, D.R. "Food Policy, Nutrition Planning, and Survival - The Cases of Kerala and Sri Lanka." *Food Policy* 4 (1979): 245-258.

Gwatkin, D.R., Wilcox, J.R., and Wray, J.D. *Can Health and Nutrition Interventions Make a Difference*? Monograph No. 13. Washington DC: Overseas Development Council, 1980.

Hall, T.L., and Mejia, A. *Health Manpower Planning: Principles, Methods, Issues.* Geneva: WHO, 1978.

Harriss, B. "Implementation of Food Distribution Policies: A Case Study in South India." *Food Policy* 8 (1983): 121-130.

Hirschhorn, N. "The Treatment of Acute Diarrhea in Children: An Historical and Physiological Perspective." *American Journal of Clinical Nutrition* 33 (1980):637-663.

ICSSR-ICMR. *Health for All - An Alternative Strategy*. Pune: Indian Institute of Education, 1981.

Jobert, B. "Populism and Health Policy: The Case of Community Health Volunteers in India." *Soc. Sci. and Med.* 20 (1985) 1-28.

Jolly, R., and King, M. "The Organization of Health Services." In *Medical Care in Developing Countries*, edited by M. King. Oxford: Oxford University Press, 1966.

Joy, J.L., and Payne, P.R. *Food and Nutrition Planning*. Rome: FAO Consultants' Report Series, No. 35, 1975.

Leslie, C. "What Caused India's Massive Community Health Workers Scheme: A Sociology of Knowledge." *Soc. Sci. and Med.* 21 (1985): 923-930.

Macagba, R.L. *Hospitals and Primary Health.* London: Intl. Hospital Fed., 1984.

Moore, G.C., and ReVelle, C. "The Hierarchical Service Location Problem." *Management Sci.* 28, 7 (1982):775-780.

Morley, D., Rohde, J. and Williams, G. *Practicing Health for All* Oxford: Oxford University Press, 1983.

Morley, D., and Woodland, M. *See How They Grow - Monitoring Child Growth for Appropriate Health Care in Developing Countries.* London: The Macmillan Press Ltd., 1979.

Mosley, W.H. "Child Survival: Research and Policy" In *Child Survival: Strategies for Research*, edited by W.H. Mosley and L.C. Chen. Cambridge: Cambridge University Press, 1984.

Pacey, A., and Payne, P., eds. *Agricultural Development and Nutrition*. London: Hutchinson, 1985.

Patel, N.R. "Locating Rural Social Service Centers in India." *Management Sci.* 25 (1979):(1)22-30.

Pebley, A.R. "Intervention Projects and the Study of Socioeconomic Determinants of Mortality." In *Child Survival: Strategies for Research*, edited by W.H. Mosley and L.C. Chen. Cambridge: Cambridge University Press, 1984.

Rahaman, M.M., Aziz, K.M.S., Munshi, M.H., Patwari, Y., and Rahman, M. "A Diarrhea Clinic in Rural Bangladesh: Influence of Distance, Age, and Sex on Attendance and Diarrheal Mortality." *Am. J. of Public Health* 72 (1982): 1124-1128.

Rifkin, S.B. *Health Planning and Community Participation: Case Studies in South-East Asia*. London:Croom-Helm, 1985.

Rushton, G. "Use of Location-Allocation Models for Improving the Geographical Accessibility of Rural Services in Developing Countries" *Intl. Regional Sci. Rev.* 9 (1984):217-240.

Scholl, E.A. "An Assessment of Community Health Workers in Nicaragua." *Soc. Sci. and Med.* 20 (1985): 207-214.

UNICEF. *The State of the World's Children 1984* New York: UNICEF, 1984.
United Nations. *Levels and Trends of Mortality Since 1950*. New York: United Nations, 1982.
Wang'ombe, J.K. "Economic Evaluation in Primary Health Care: The Case of Western Kenya Community Based Health Care Projects." *Soc. Sci. and Med.* 18 (1984):375-385.
WHO-UNICEF. *Primary Health Care - Report of the International Conference on Primary health Care, Alma Ata, USSR*. Geneva, 1978.
World Health Organization. *The Global Eradication of Smallpox: Final Report of the Global Commission for the Certification of Smallpox Eradication*. Geneva:WHO, 1980.

OPERATIONAL FEASIBILITY ANALYSIS OF PUBLIC SERVICES IN DEVELOPING COUNTRIES

Israel Prion

The term 'Integrated Regional Development (IRD) Planning' indicates a parallel, simultaneous, correlated and coordinated planning of the three main economic sectors: agriculture, industry and services. Because of this specific, intersectoral nature of IRD planning, many planners tried to develop a common analysis method for the three economic sectors, that can be used for the selection of the best planning alternatives, for the regional economy as a whole and for each of the economic sectors.

Till now, regional development planners succeeded in implementing this idea in the sectoral planning of the primary and secondary sectors, but failed to use it in the tertiary sector. In order to understand this problem, we need to review the target definitions of planning at the macro and micro levels.

At the macro level, the major development planning target is usually the maximization of regional income expressed in terms of GNP or GPD. This target is quite adequate for the macro-planning of the primary and the secondary sectors, but does not apply to the the planning of the services sector, and is particularly invalid for the planning of public services. The major part (80-90 percent) of GDP in public services usually comes from wages and salaries. The share of net income in the GDP of public services is insignificant. Any maximization of GDP in the services sector is actually a maximization of wages and salaries, in other words - maximization of expenditures, and therefore inacceptable as a development target.

At the micro-level, planning of the primary and secondary sectors is based on methods of economic analysis, such as cost/benefit analysis or internal rate of return, that enable the planner to evaluate project alternatives by profitability. The cost/benefit ratio is a significant index for evaluating the feasibility of development projects, since it enables us to computerize the returns of each unit of additional invested capital. The higher this ratio, the more viable is the development project since the net return of the investment is higher. The internal rate of return on the other hand, determines the maximum interest rate which a development project is capable of sustaining. The calculation of both indices is based on the estimation of running expenses and parallel income, for each year of the implementation, using mainly the discounted cash flow analysis techniques.

This methodology cannot be recommended for public services planning, since there is no way to evaluate the direct economic benefits of public services, such as the direct contribution of a new vocational school, a rural clinic, etc. to the GDP. Although the composition of an annual cost flow, including the schedule of initial investment, cost of capital renewals and direct costs of production, can be estimated in public services, it is impossible to express the composition of the gross benefits flow of public services, i.e., annual gross returns. As a result, there is a no benefit criteria for the evaluation of project alternatives as far as allocation of manpower and capital in public services is considered.

To date, there have been a few unsuccessful attempts to estimate the indirect benefits of public services in a planned area, and, at the present state of the art one cannot expect a substantial progress in this direction. A better way to solve this problem is to try and develop a specific evaluation scheme for projects of public service, as suggested in the following.

PLANNING OF PUBLIC SERVICES IN DEVELOPMENT AREAS

It is still an accepted practice to regard investment capital in the services as a 'bottleneck,' and to determine the practicability of a given project by the success of the passage through it. But this is not the case. A public service facility may remain closed, even if it was 'contributed' by one of the assistance agencies, as long as the community is unable to secure the necessary funds to finance its share in the operation expenses. At times, the cost of operating such a facility (an elementary or high school, a clinic, hospital, etc.) for two consecutive years may equal the amount needed to establish it. Furthermore, annual operating costs constitute an immediate and current expenditure, whereas payments on the account of the invested capital are distributed along a relatively large number of years. Consequently, the ability of the recipient population to shoulder the onus of the yearly costs, determines the starting point for the planning of the public services system. In other words not a 'textbook norm' determines the planning of public services, but rather a programming of these services as a function of the users' income level anticipated at the target year of the regional development plan.

This assertion means that we have to abandon the widespread practice of planning public services according to standard norms, which too often rest upon theoretical and unrealistic considerations. Thus, for instance, the generally recommended norm of hospital beds in developing countries is 4 beds per 1,000 inhabitants, but I know from my experience in Latin America and Africa, that such a norm cannot be implemented in most developing regions in the next 10 to 15 years. Usually, the indication of feasibility studies is that a reasonable norm should be reduced to half the former estimate (i.e. 2 beds per 1,000 inhabitants).

The planner of services in developing areas should therefore figure out in advance his own normative criteria (relating to the extent and standard of public services), to match the size of the contributions by official agencies on the one hand and the expected income level of the population on the other. These norms are bound to be different in various regions for different reasons.

The approach to the planning of public services and its methodology merit a detailed discussion, which cannot be included here. We will only mention that the operational feasibility study is made up of three steps. The interdisciplinary planning team begins its work by an early program for the public services: the elements of the schooling system in the region, the distribution of the pupil population among the schools as a percentage of all the children of relevant ages, study directions, etc, on the basis of desirability and apparent feasibility. Guided by these outlines, economic planners calculate the average operation cost of the educational services for one family in the region, starting from elementary school, through high school and vocational education. The final step examines the possibilities to finance the overall operation expenses of the educational system at the target year of the plan.

Part of the expenditure required to operate the educational system will be provided by official agencies, and data from the 'National Accounts' may serve as an estimate for the magnitude of the potential contribution by the government (as a percentage of the GNP). The rest of the costs must be born by the population (private consumption expenditures). If the estimate of the annual average expenses for education per family does not exceed a reasonable rate of the expenditures for private consumption, the plan can be considered implementable. But if the expenses turn out to be considerably larger compared to the rate used in the 'consumption basket' of populations with a similar income level, the plan is probably too ambitious and should be returned to the drawing table for reconsideration and cuts. Feasibility studies for other public services (health etc.) will be performed in a similar manner.

By substituting the normative services planning with the operational feasibility analysis planners are able to estimate flexible norms and standards of public services, in accordance to the income targets of the regional development plans at different stages of development.

METHODOLOGY OF OPERATIONAL FEASIBILITY ANALYSIS OF PUBLIC SERVICES IN DEVELOPING COUNTRIES

From the methodology point of view the operational feasibility analysis of public services is divided into four stages, as follows:

1. Designing a model of the spatial organization in the planned region simultaneously with a hierarchical model of public services (education, health).

2. Preparing operational cost calculations for different systems of public services (education, health).

3. Estimating the reasonable budgets needed for the operation of public services.

4. Determining the volume and standards of public services by balancing operational costs and budgets.

The methodology was applied in several places (1); in the following we present the concrete case of the Zomba-Machinga Region in Malawi.(2)

FIRST STAGE

The design of the spatial organization model is based on three principles:

Accessibility, or optimum territorial dispersal of the services, in order to reach many small producers scattered over a wide area with little or no transportation facilities;

Efficiency of services in terms of prices and quality; and

Concentration of services which operate at the same level in certain well-defined locations.

The spatial organization model for the Zomba-Machinga Region was therefore designed to include villages, rural centres, sub-regional centres and a regional centre (see Figure 1). In general, the location and extent of services follow fairly closely the distribution, size and requirements of the population at different hierarchical levels of the Zomba-Machinga Region.

Estimates of the average population in the different centres of the Zomba-Machinga region were as follows:

- A village - 650 persons (150 families).
- Rural centre - 5,000 persons or 1,000 families (the population of the rural centre and the villages attached to it).
- Sub-regional centre - 42,000 persons or 8,400 families, 28.5 percent of them urban and 71.5 percent - rural (in the sub-regional town and in all the rural centres and villages attached to it).
- Regional centre - 1,240,600 persons or 248,120 families (all the population foreseen in the region in the target year of the plan).

Figure 1. Conceptual Model of the Spatial Organization and Hierarchy of Public Services in the Zomba-Machinga Region

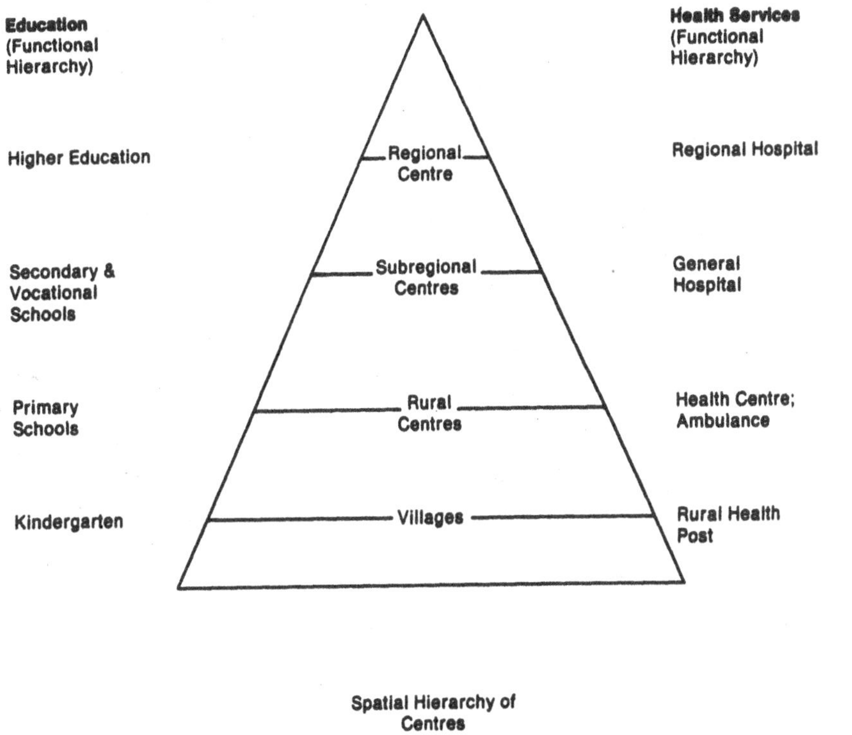

SECOND STAGE

We have already mentioned that an interdisciplinary planning team outlines an early programme for the development of the educational and health systems on the basis of desirability and apparent feasibility. The calculations of operation, guided by these directives, estimate the average annual expenditures for the operation of public services per family. It examines the average basic investment for each service unit (for education: kindergarten, primary school, etc.), the annual operation expenses, the number of persons employed in each unit of service, the total value added, the value added per employee, etc., (see Appendix 1 to 4). By means of a similar methodology economic planners calculate the average operation costs of health and other services per family in the region (see Appendix 5 to 8). The estimated average expenditures per family in the target year for each level of the education and health services are presented in Tables 1 and 2.

THIRD STAGE

The operating budget for public services is financed by the government and the private sector.

At present the Government of Malawi spends 1.66 percent of the GNP on education; it is estimated that by the target year this support will be increased to 2 percent. It is recommended that the government should apportion its education budget as follows: 1.8 percent of the average GNP/family for the primary sector and 0.7 percent for other sectors. The remainder of the budget, 0.2 and 1.3 percent of the GNP per family in the primary and other sectors, respectively, should be directed by the government to other fields of education, namely adult education, universities, etc).

Table 1: Estimated Average Annual Expenditure (KW)* on Educational Services per Family (1996)

Services	Sector 1	Sectors 2 & 3	Average
Kindergarten	-	2.0	-
Primary School	33.5	33.5	33.50
Secondary School	4.5	13.4	8.95
Vocational School	5.6	16.8	11.20
Total	43.6	65.7	53.65

*1 KW = US$1.1 (1982).

Note: It was assumed that the participation of children in secondary and vocational schools would be much higher in the urban population (Sectors 2 and 3), than in rural areas (15% vs. 5% of the age groups). The result is a much higher estimated average annual expenditure per urban family.

Table 2: Estimated Average Annual Expenditure (KW) on Health Services per Family 1996

Services	Sector 1	Sectors 2 and 3
Rural Health Post	2.9	0
Health Sub-centre	6.8	6.8
General Hospital	25.7	25.7
Ambulance	1.6	2.4
Total	37.0	34.9

The government of Malawi is now spending 0.86 percent of the GNP on health services. It is estimated that an additional 1.0 percent of the GNP will be allocated to health services by the target year. It is reasonable for the government to discriminate between rural and urban sectors in regard to its contribution to health facilities, since the VA per family is considerably less in the rural sector (1.5 percent of the GNP per capita) than in the urban sector (0.3 percent of the GNP per capita for the urban sector).

Table 3 shows the estimated average government spending per family on education and health services in 1996.

Table 3: Estimated Government Spending in 1996 (KW)

Sector	Foreseen GNP at the National Level in 1996		Foreseen Government Expenditures per Family in 1996	
	Per capita	Per family	% of GNP	KW
Education				
1	360	1,800	1.8	32.4
2 and 3	360	1,800	0.7	12.6
Health Services				
1	360	1,800	1.5	27.0
2 and 3	360	1,800	0.3	5.4

The remaining expenses and health service expenses have to be paid by the population (private consumption expenditures). According to various publications, private expenditures for education in countries with per capita income level equal to that envisaged in the region in 1996 constitute some 4 percent of the private consumption expenditure.(3) The parallel index for health services is 3 to 3.5 percent of private consumption expenditures. A summary of the population contribution (private consumption expenditures) to the operation of public services is presented in Table 4.

Table 4: Private Consumption Expenditure (PCE) per Family on Education and Health Services (1996)

Sector	VA per Family According to the Plan*	PCE per Family		PCE Expenditures per Family for Public Services	
		% of GNP*	Total (KW)	% of PCE	Total (KW)
Education					
1	400	75	300	4.0	12.0
2 and 3	2,431	60	1,459	4.0	58.4
Health Services					
1	400	75	300	3.5	10.5
2 and 3	2,431	60	1,459	3.0	43.8

*Data estimated at the previous planning stage of IRD (the so-called 'regional macro-planning').

FOURTH STAGE

If the average estimate of the annual expenses per family for public services does not exceed the estimate of the budget, the proposed volume and standards of services may be considered implementable. Table 5 presents the balance between the estimated cost and budget for education and health services, showing that in this case the plan is indeed implementable. When the cost is considerably larger than the budget, the plan should be returned to the planning team for another iteration of the operational feasibility analysis.

Table 5: Cost/Budget Balance for Operating Educational and Health Services (1996)

Sector	Cost (KW)	Budget					Balance (Cost as % of budget) KW
		Government Expenditure		PCE Expenditures		Total KW	
		%	KW	%	KW		
Education							
1	43.6	73.0	32.4	27.0	12.0	44.4	98.2
2 and 3	65.7	17.7	12.6	82.3	58.4	71.0	92.5
Health Services							
1	37.0	72.0	27.0	28.0	10.5	37.5	98.7
2 and 3	34.9	11.0	5.4	89.0	43.8	49.2	71.0

On the basis of the aforestated, the service planner in a developing region should figure out pertinent planning indices which are confirmed by the operational feasibility analysis (Table 6).

Table 6: Planning Indices for the Zomba-Machinga Region in Malawi, Confirmed by the Operational Feasibility Analysis

Service Branch Education	Kinder-garten	Primary School	Secondary School	Vocational School
Location	All levels of spatial hierarchy	Rural, sub-regional & regional centers	Subregional and regional centers	
Rate of population served (%):				
- rural	-	95	5	5
- urban	15	95	15	15
No. of children/classroom	30-35	45	40	40
No. of shifts	1	2	2	2
Level of education (years)	2	*8	4	4
Employees classroom:				
1) shifts	1.5	-	-	-
2) shifts	-	2.46	3.5	4.17
Annual depreciation (%):				
- Construction	2	4	2	2
- Equipment	15	15	15	15
Average VA/employee (KW)	666	889	2,387	2,518
Miscellaneous expenditures as % of total expenditure	15	15	15	15
Area of construction per classroom (m^2)	50	60	80	90
Average cost of construction (KW per 1 m^2)	**40	**40	80	90

* Five years of compulsory education; it is supposed that 50 percent of the children will continue in the last 3 years of primary education.
**Cost of construction materials only (built in the framework of self-help)

Obviously the numerical expression of these indices will vary for different countries and regions, according to the planned levels of development and income. Right now there are not enough development projects with operational feasibility analysis to have a sufficiently big sample for statistical analysis of development trends in this field. However, some conclusions can be made by analysing the existing projects as shown in Table 7.

Table 7: Some Results of the Operational Feasibility Analysis at Different Levels of Regional Development

Region	GDP/CAP (KW)	Enrollment (% of age group) Kinder-garten*	Secondary School**	Vocational School**	Hospital (Beds/ 1000 inh.)	Ambulance (No./ 1000 inh.)
Zomba-Machinga (Malawi)	200	15	5-15	5-15	1.80	15,000
Region Sur (Dominican Republic)	800	18	15-20	20-25	2.20	10,000
Heutar Atlantica (Costa Rica)	1,100	20	20-25	25-30	2.35	8,000

* In urban areas
**The left column refers to rural areas and the right column to urban areas

The size and standard of the public services increase with the level of income per capita. We assume that the population served is entitled to the best public services, but the actual level of public services will be determined by the financial ability to operate them. The operational feasibility analysis is based on the estimated national income level - on the one hand, and on the regional income on the other. As a result, the operational feasibility analysis is a link between the services sector and the rest of the economic sectors within the framework of integrated regional development planning in developing countries.

NOTES

1. The methodology of the Operational Feasibility Analysis was applied in a number of regional development projects presented in the following publications: I. Prion et al. *Proyecto de Planificacion del Desarrollo Regional Integral - Perija, Estado Zulia, Venezuela* (CINDER, Maracaibo and CERUR, Rehovot, 1977.) I. Prion et al. *Lampang Region - Thailand: An Integrated Rural Development Project* (SSC Rehovot, 1980). I. Prion et al. *Proyecto de Planificacion del Desarrollo Rural Integral de la Region Guanare-Masparro (Venezuela)* (CERUR, Rehovot, 1980). I. Prion et al. *Proyecto de Planificacion - Region Sur, Republica Dominicana* (CERUR, Rehovot, 1981). D. Pelley et al. *Planning Project Nakuru-Nyandarua Region - Kenya* (SSC, Rehovot, 1982). I. Prion et al. *Winneba-Swedru Region - Ghana: An Integrated Rural Development Project* (SSC, Rehovot, 1982). I. Prion et al. *Proyecto de Planificacion del Desarrollo Rural Integrado de la Region PACOSAN - Peru* (CERUR, Rehovot, 1982). D. Pelley et al. *Planning Project - Zomba and Machinga Districts - Malawi* (SSC, Rehovot, 1983). I. Prion et al. *Proyecto de Planificacion - Region Bolivar, Ecuador* (CERUR, Rehovot, 1984). I. Prion et al. *Proyecto de Planificacion - Region CALVO-SILES, Boliva* (CERUR, Rehovot, 1984). I. Prion et al. *Proyecto de Desarrollo Rural Integrado de la Region Huetar Altantica y el Canton Talamanca, Costa Rica* (CERUR, Rehovot, 1986).

2. D. Pelley & I. Prion et al. *Planning Project - Zomba and Machinga Districts, Malawi* (SSC, Rehovot, 1983).

3. S. Kuznets, *Modern Economic Growth Rate, Structure and Spread.* (New Haven: Yale Univ. Press, 1969). Kuznets claims that private expenditure on education, recreation and amusement, at a similar level of income, constitutes about 5 percent of private consumption.

APPENDICES

Appendix 1: Annual Operation Cost of a Kindergarten in an Urban Neighborhood

1.	Population served: 12,000 persons or 2,400 families	
2.	No. of children in each age-group: - Urban sector 15% x 12,000 x 3.8%* = 68 minus 5% (mentally or physically retarded): - Children per classroom:	 65 pupils 30 to 35
3.	No. of schools: 1; No. of directions: 1; Years of education: 2	
4.	No. of classrooms:	4
5.	Constructed area (50 m^2/classroom):	200 m^2
6.	No. employees	6
7.	Total investment (KW): - Construction (KW8/m^2): - Equipment (15% of construction):	18,400 16,000 2,400
8.	Operation expenditure: - Total depreciation (KW): 680 (Construction 2% - 320**; Equipment 15% - 360) - Salaries and Wages: **3,317 - Miscellaneous (15% of total) 705 - Total Expenditure 4,702	
9.	Expenditure per family in the urban sector: 4,702/2,400 = 2.0 KW	
10.	Total Value Added (KW): 680 + 3,317 = 3,997 Value Added per employee (KW): 3,997/6 = 666	

* The calculation of enrollment rate is as follows:

Birthrate -	4.2%
Mortality rate -	1.1% (0.4% till the age of school + 0.7% adults)
Natural Growth Rate -	3.1%
Enrollment rate:	4.2% - 0.4% = 3.8%

**The calculation of salaries and wages (KW):

4 Teachers x 600 =	2,400
2 Others x 140 =	280
Sub-total	2,680
Target year of planning (+10%)	2,948
Social Security (12.5%)	369
Total in target year	3,317

Appendix 2: Annual Operation Cost of a Primary School in a Rural Centre (1KW = US$1.1 (1982))

1. Population served: 5,000 persons or 1,000 families
   - Urban population: 500 persons or 100 families
   - Rural population: 4,500 persons or 900 families
2. Children in each age-group:
   - Urban sector
     (500 x 3.8%) minus 5% mentally or physically retarded: 18
   - Rural sector
     (4,500 x 3.8%) minus 5% mentally or physically retarded: 162
   - Total (urban and rural): 180
   - No. of children per classroom: 45 (one shift)
3. No. of schools: 1; No. of directions: 2; Years of education: 8
4. No. of classrooms: 13 (2 shifts)*
5. Constructed area (60 m^2/class): 780 m^2
6. No. employees: 32
7. Total investment: KW35,880
   - Construction (KW40/m^2): KW31,200
   - Equipment (15% of construction): KW4,680
8. Operation expenditure:
   - Total depreciation: KW2,418;
     (Construction - KW1,248; Equipment - KW1,170)
   - Salaries and wages: **KW26,031
   - Miscellaneous (15% of total) KW5,020
   - Total Expenditure KW33,469
9. Expenditure per family in urban sector : KW33.5
   Expenditure per family in rural sector: KW33.5
10. Total value added: KW28,449
    Value added per employee: KW889

* 180/45 = 4 classrooms for one age group (one shift); first five years of education are compulsory, therefore 4 classrooms x 5 = 20 classrooms (one shift); or 20/2 shifts = 10 classrooms (two shifts).
It is expected that only 50% of the pupils will continue through the last 3 years of primary education, therefore 90/45 = 2 classrooms x 3 years = 6 classrooms (one shift); or 6 classrooms/2 shifts = 3 classrooms (two shifts); total No. of classrooms required = 10+3=13 classrooms (two shifts).

**Salaries and Wages (in KW)

1 Headmaster x 1,000	1,000
13 x 2 Teachers/classroom x 735	19,110
1 Secretary x 365	365
4 Others x 140	560
Sub-total	21,035
Target year of planning (+10%)	23,139
Social Security (12.5%)	2,892
Total in target year	26,031

Appendix 3: Annual Operation Cost of a Secondary School in a Sub-Regional Centre

1. Population served: 42,000 persons or 8,400 families
   - Urban: 12,000 persons or 2,400 families
   - Rural: 30,000 persons or 6,000 families
2. Children in each age-group:
   - Urban sector 15% x 12,000 x 3.8% = 68 minus 5% (mentally or physically retarded: 65 pupils)
   - Rural sector 5% x 30,000 x 3.8% = 57 minus 5% (mentally or physically retarded: 54 pupils)
   - Total 119 pupils
   - Children per classroom: 40
3. No. of schools: 1; No. of directions: 3; Years of education: 4
4. No. of classrooms: 6 (2 shifts)
5. Constructed area (80 m^2/class): 480 m^2
6. No. of employees: 21

7.	Total investment:	KW44,160
	- Construction (KW80/m^2):	KW38,400
	- Equipment (15% of construction):	KW5,760
8.	Operation expenditure: total depreciation: KW1,632 (construction 2% - 768, equipment 15% - 864)	
	- Salaries and wages:	*48,492
	- Miscellaneous (15% of total):	8,845
	- Total Expenditure:	58,969
9.	Expenditure in urban sector (54.6%):	32,197
	Expenditure in rural sector (45.4%):	26,772
	Expenditure per family in urban sector:	13.4
	Expenditure per family in rural sector:	4.5
10.	Total Value Added:	50,214
	Value Added per employee:	2,387

* The calculation of salaries and wages (KW):

1 Headmaster x 3,100	3,100
6 x 2.5 teachers/classroom x 2,480	34,720
1 Nurse x 440	440
1 Secretary x 365	365
4 Others x 140	560
Subtotal	39,185
Target year of planning (+10%)	43,104
Social Security (12.5%)	5,388
Total target year	48,492

Appendix 4: Annual Operation Cost of a Vocational School in a Sub-Regional Centre

1.	Population served:	42,000 persons or 8,400 families
	- Urban:	12,000 persons or 2,400 families
	- Rural:	30,000 persons or 6,000 families
2.	Children in each age-group:	
	- Urban sector 15% x 12,000 x 3.8% = 68 minus 5% (mentally or physically retarded: 65)	
	- Rural sector 1.5% x 30,000 x 3.8% = 57 minus 5% (mentally or physically retarded: 54)	
	- Total 119	
	- Children per classroom: 40	
3.	No. of schools: 1; No. of directions: 3; Years of education: 4	
4.	No. of classrooms:	6 (2 shifts)
5.	Constructed area (90 m^2 per class): 540 m^2	
6.	No. of employees:	25
7.	Total investment	KW47,250
	- Construction (KW70/m^2):	37,800
	- Equipment (25% of construction):	9,450
8.	Operational expenditure:	
	- Total Depreciation	2,174
	(Construction 2% - 756, Equipment 15% - 1,418)	
	- Salaries and wages	60,768
	- Miscellaneous (15% of total)	11,107
	- Total expenditures	KW74,049
9.	Expenditure in urban sector (54.6%)	KW40,431
	Expenditure in rural sector(45.4%)	33,618
	Expenditure per family in urban sector	16.8
	Expenditure per family in rural sector	5.6
10.	Total Value Added:	KW62,942
	Value Added per Employee:	KW2,518

*The calculation of Salaries and Wages (KW):

1 Headmaster x 3,100	3,100
6 x 3.2 Teachers/class x 2,480	44,640
1 Nurse x 440	440
1 Secretary x 365	365
4 Others x 140	560
Sub-total	49,105
Target year of planning (+10%)	54,016
Social Security (12.5%)	6,752
Total in target year	60,768

Appendix 5: Annual Operation Cost of a Rural Health Post in One of Two Villages (population of 750 each)

1.	Population served:	1,500 persons or 300 families
2.	Constructed area ($50m^2$):	50 m^2
3.	Total investment:	KW2,300
	- Construction ($KW40/m^2$):	KW2,000
	- Equipment (15% of construction):	KW300
4.	No. of employees:	1
5.	Operation expenditure:	
	- Total depreciation: KW125 (Construction 4% - 80; Equipment 15% - 45)	
	- Salaries and wages:	*KW620
	- Miscellaneous (15% of total)	130
	- Total expenditures	KW875
6.	Average expenditure per family	KW2.9
7.	Total Value Added	KW745

*The calculation of salaries and wages (KW):

1 Homecraft worker x 500	500
Target year of planning (+10%)	550
Social Security (12.5%)	70
Total in the target year	620

Appendix 6: Annual Operation Cost of a Health Sub-Center in Each Rural Center (serving the population attached to it or in an urban neighborhood of 5,000 inhabitants)

1.	Population served:	5,000 persons or 1,000 families
2.	Constructed area:	120 m^2
3.	Total investment:	KW5,760
	-Construction ($KW40/m^2$):	KW4,800
	-Equipment (20% of construction):	KW960
4.	No. of employees:	6
5.	Operation expenditures:	
	- Total depreciation: KW432 (Construction 4% - 192; Equipment 25% - 240)	
	- Salaries and wages:	*KW5,037
	- Miscellaneous (20% of total):	KW1,367
	- Total expenditure:	KW6,836
6.	Average expenditure per family: 6,836/1,000 = KW6.8	
7.	Total Value Added:	KW5,469
	Value Added/employee:	KW911.5

* The calculation of salaries and wages (KW):

1 Nurse x 890	890
2 Medical assistants x 1,090	2,180
1 Homecraft worker x 500	500
2 Service workers x 250	500
Sub-total	4,070
Target year of planning (+10%)	4,477
Social Security (12.5%)	560
Total in the Target Year	5,037

Appendix 7: Annual Operation Cost of a General Hospital in a Sub-Regional Center (serving all rural centers and villages attached to it)

1.	Population served: 42,000 persons or 8,400 families	
2.	No. of beds (2 per 1,000 inhabitants	84
3.	Area of construction ($40m^2$ per bed):	3,360 m^2
4.	Total Investment:	KW453,600
	- Construction ($KW100/m^2$):	KW336,000
	- Equipment (35% of construction):	KW117,600
5.	No. of employees:	87
6.	Operational Expenditure:	
	- Total Depreciation: KW24,360 (Construction (2%) - 6,720; Equipment (15%) - 17,640)	
	- Salaries and wages:	*KW115,756
	- Miscellaneous (35% of total):	KW75,447
	Total expenditure:	KW215,563
7.	Average expenditure per family:	KW25.7
8.	Value Added:	
	- Total:	KW140,116
	- Per employee:	KW1,610.5

*Salaries and Wages

0.04 Doctors/bed KW5,700 x 3	17,100
0.25 Nurses/bed KW890 x 21	18,690
0.6 Assistants/bed KW1,090 x 50	54,500
0.16 service workers/bed KW250 x 13	3,250
Sub-total	93,540
Target year of planning (+10%)	102,894
Social Security (12.5%)	12,862
Total in target year	115,756

Appendix 8: Annual Operation Cost of an Ambulance (serving 3 rural centers or 15,000 and 10,000 inhabitants in an urban neighborhood)

1.	Population served:	
	- Rural:	15,000 inhabitants or 3,000 families
	- Urban:	10,000 inhabitants or 2,000 families
2.	Constructed area:	20 m^2
3.	Total investment:	KW15,500
	-Construction (KW25/m^2):	KW500
	-Ambulance with equipment:	KW15,000
4.	No. of employees:	2
5.	Operation expenditures:	
	- Total depreciation: KW2,270	
	(Construction 4% - 20; Equipment 15% - 2,250)	
	- Salaries and wages:	*1,485
	- Miscellaneous:	1,000
	- Total expenditure:	KW4,755
6.	Average expenditure per family:	
	rural =	KW1.6
	urban =	KW2.4
7.	Total Value Added:	KW3,755
	Value Added per employee	KW1,878

* The calculation of salaries and wages (KW):

2 Ambulance drivers x 600	1,200
Sub-total	1,200
Target year of planning (+10%)	1,320
Social Security (12.5%)	165
Total in the Target Year	1,485

Part 4: Regional Industrialization

AN APPROACH TO GROWTH PATTERNS IN REGIONAL INDUSTRIALIZATION

Raphael Bar-El

INTRODUCTION: A GENERAL APPROACH

Industrial planning usually involves a static, 'freeze frame' analysis, in which planners look at a region at a specific time and prescribe a development plan using the static existing or expected situation as a basis for decision making. I claim that industrialization of a region should be considered as a continuously changing process, the characteristics of which vary according to the stages of development and the external conditions in the region and the country. The general approach suggested here is based on the assumption that the role of industry in the process of regional/rural development affects the patterns of growth in the region and is affected by them. Industrial development should therefore be continuously adapted to the changing conditions in the region. Some of these conditions are externally imposed, while others are generated by the industrial development process itself. Fig. 1 illustrates in a very schematic way the relations between industrial development and these two groups of variables.

Figure 1. A Schematic Illustration of the Relations Between Industrial Policy and the Endogenous and Exogenous Variables

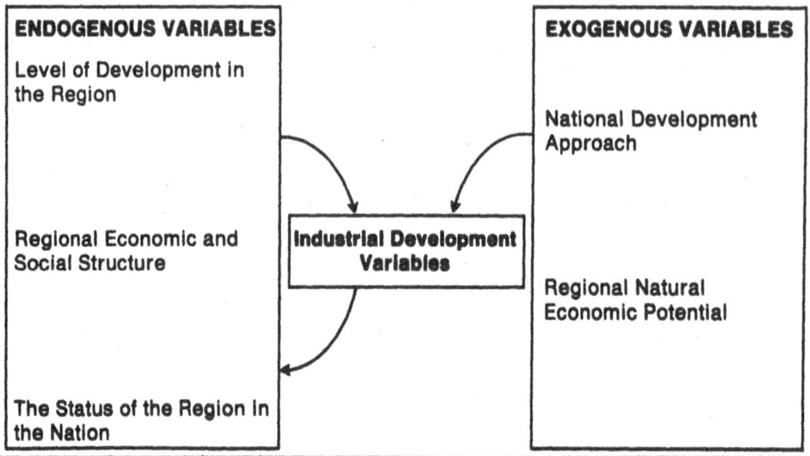

Endogenous variables represent the characteristics of a region which both influence industrial development and are influenced by it, namely: 1) the level of development in the region; 2) the regional economic and social infrastructure; and 3) the position of the region in relation to the nation as a whole. Exogenous variables represent factors in the region which affect industrial policy but are virtually not affected by it, namely the national development policy and the natural economic potential of the region.

THE DEFINITION OF INDUSTRIAL DEVELOPMENT

The first question to arise is what industrial strategy should be employed to achieve the optimal results at different levels of development within the region, given the various external influences? For example, should we select labor-intensive manufacturing plants and small scale industries which require low skilled workers and produce products for the local market or would it be more effective to adopt a different strategy which encourages large scale, highly mechanized more capital intensive production offering higher skilled employment, and producing for the national market or for export?

In order to address this question, we should first define the main components of industrial development strategy, and determine the most important characteristics of the industrial activity which can be used to define industrial strategy. To make such a definition, we shall classify the components of industrial strategy into three groups: (1) variables related to the production process; (2) variables related to the product characteristics; and (3) variables related to the spatial characteristics of industrial development.

VARIABLES RELATED TO THE PRODUCTION PROCESS

The production process may be considered from three aspects. The first is capital-intensity of the production process as it may be measured by capital per worker (or by the capital-output ratio); this indicates the level of technology or mechanization used in the manufacturing process. The second aspect may be defined as the human capital intensity, as indicated by the level of skills required by the manufacturing plant. (1) The third aspect is the scale of operation in the manufacturing plants, measured by size generally in terms of number of employees, or - in some cases - in terms of the scope of production or sales.(2)

VARIABLES RELATED TO PRODUCT CHARACTERISTICS

The characteristics of the industrial product may also be grouped into three classes of components. The first is the type of product represented by the type of industrial branch (using international standard industrial classifications). One important classification uses the income elasticity of demand for the product, and distinguishes between products for 'mass consumption' at relatively low income levels and 'high income' products.(3) The second is the market for the specific product under consideration: local, regional, national or export. Whereas the first and second components measure the characteristics of a specific industrial product, the third component relates to the composition of the whole manufacturing output in the region, and measures the degree of its diversity versus specialization. A high degree of specialization would imply a concentration of most manufacturing activity of the region in one or in a few products, while diversity is achieved when the manufacturing activity involves a wide range of products.

VARIABLES RELATED TO THE SPATIAL CHARACTERISTICS

Again we may refer to three major components. The first relates to the spatial patterns of backward and forward linkages of industrial development: who are the suppliers to the manufacturing plants and the buyers of its products and where are they located?(4) We also characterize plants by their main locational factors, such as proximity to markets, to raw materials, to labor-force supply etc.(5)

The third component relates to the spatial hierarchy of manufacturing activities in the region and on the national level. When such hierarchy does not exist the industrial structure would be based on plants with strong local backward and forward linkages. The existence of a hierarchical structure would be indicated by linkages at various spatial levels (as a function of the type of plant), resulting in higher integration of manufacturing activities into the economy of the region and the nation.(6)

INDUSTRIALIZATION AND THE ENDOGENOUS PROCESS OF DEVELOPMENT

The first and most important group of variables to be considered in this context is the level of development in the region (see Fig. 1). The significance of this group to industrialization (7) is reflected by demand for industrial products and supply of production factors, (see Fig. 2). Rising levels of income and development in the region cause changes in both. The demand for industrial products increases, creating more opportunities for industrial development, and the composition of such products shifts from agricultural or food industry products more to non-food industrial products.(8) Even within total non-food demand, the type of consumption changes as development approaches higher levels - away from necessities and less sophisticated products to more technologically advanced goods. Such changes in the composition of demand provide a basis for more diversified industrial activities, including more advanced industrial plants.

As far as supply is concerned, a rise in the level of regional development alters the two major factors of production: capital and labor. Shifts in capital result mainly from an increase in saving rate and by higher absolute capital accumulation, and allow the establishment of more technologically advanced industries for which no financing was available before. Thus, at high levels of development and lower rates of income expenditure on necessities, the saving potential of the population increases the potential for investment in new industrial activities.(9)

The improvement in labor skills, education and health (or human capital) that results from the development process is no less important than the accumulation of financial capital. Higher level of knowledge and professional skills enable the adoption of more sophisticated industrial activities which otherwise could not operate in the region.(10)

In summary, it seems that as development advances changes in supply are complementary to changes in demand, demand for new types of products is accompanied by an increasing ability of the production factors to meet the new needs in terms of capital, skills and technology.(11)

The second group of endogenous variables which help define the endogenous process of development is the regional economic and social infrastructure. In general, this may be defined as the ability of the region to serve as the site of industrial economic activity. This ability is characterized first by the economic and physical infrastructure in the region, namely the quality of roads, power, water and sewage systems, suitable industrial sites and communication network. These are the basic necessities which an industry generally requires to operate in a region, and they improve as the level of development in the region increases. Another subcomponent is the social infrastructure in the region, mainly the quality of living which includes the availability and quality of housing, health services, education network and other social services.(12) The third component involves the organizational and social patterns in the region. At higher levels of income the aspirations are usually for more challenging and advanced jobs than at lower income levels, when the labor force is willing to accept less skilled employment. Also important is the attitude

Figure 2. Major Components of the Endogenous Process of Development

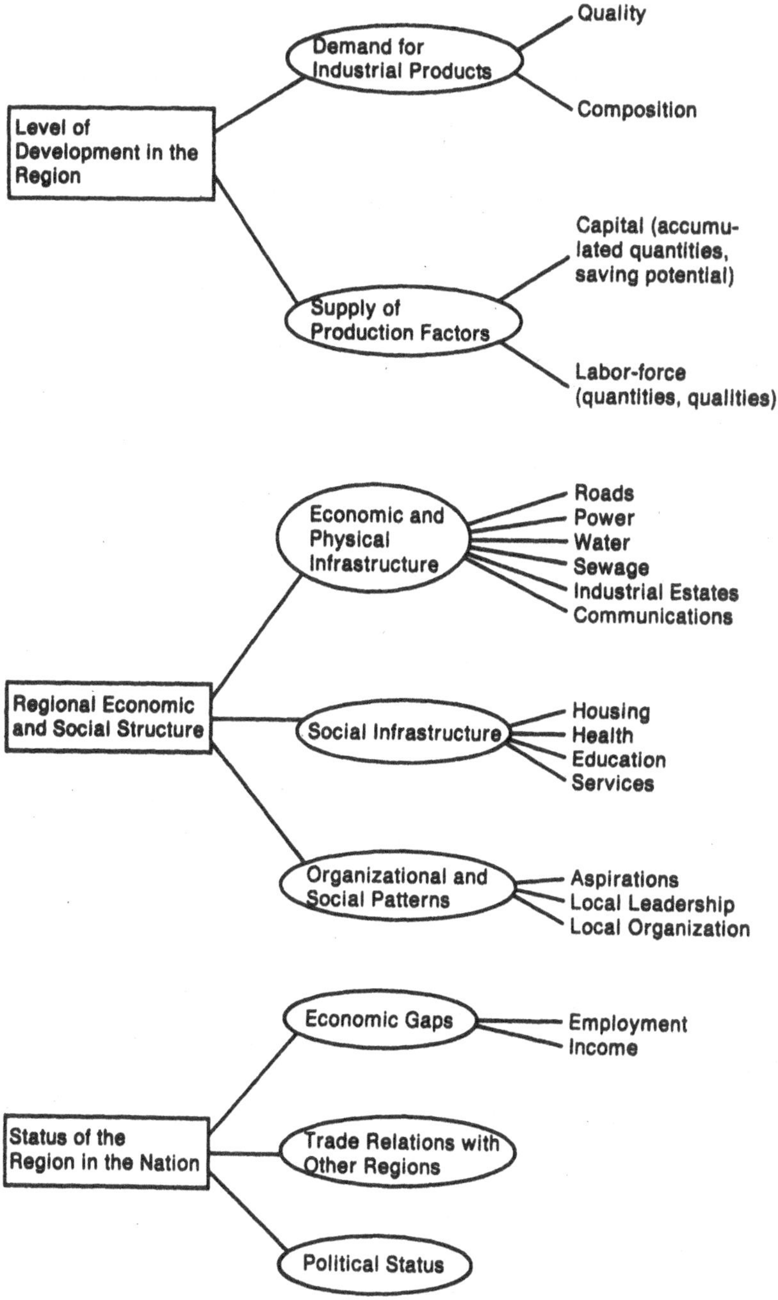

of local leadership (political, religious or educational) toward industrialization and the development process in the region.

On the whole, the importance of the regional structure is a result of the natural tendencies of manufacturing to concentrate.(13) The first trends of industrial decentralization have been attributed to changes in regional structure and characteristics.(14) A process of regional industrial development is therefore highly dependent on the regional structure.(15)

The relation between the region and the nation represents the third group of endogenous variables, and is represented by three aspects: economic gaps, trade relations with other regions, and political status. Economic gaps between regions (in terms of production, income and employment levels), as well as the volume and quality of trade relations indicate the extent of isolation from or integration with economic processes in the nation. The political power of a region, represented by its electoral weight or economic strength, may determine the allocation of resources for its industrial development. All of these factors influence the region's ability to generate a process of industrialization and development, and to become integrated into the economy of the nation as a whole. As the stage of development advances, we may witness a stronger relation between the region and the nation and stronger links between the industrial development of the region and that of the nation.

A CLASSIFICATION OF ENDOGENOUS TYPOLOGIES

Using all the variables presented above which represent various aspects of the endogenous process of development, we may theoretically define an endless number of profiles of regions at given points in time, each one of them having specific implications regarding the kind of industrial policy that should be adopted. For example, one profile can be defined by an extremely low level of development in the region expressed by a low demand for industrial products, low levels of skills and education and scarcity of capital (first sub-group of endogenous variables); a reasonably acceptable physical infrastructure, a weak social infrastructure and strong organizational patterns (second sub-group); and marked discrepancies between the region and the country as a whole (third sub-group). In another profile all the characteristics may be similar excluding one (for example, a stronger social infrastructure). In this way, we may define a very large number of profiles, resulting in a very large number of potential industrial policies.

In reality, the actual number of profiles may be smaller than the number of theoretical combinations. One important reason is probably the existence of strong correlations between variables; for example, it is most probable to expect a strong social infrastructure in a region where the physical infrastructure is well developed.

For the purposes of this paper, and for the sake of simplification, I propose to classify all endogenous typologies roughly into three groups: low, middle and high level of development. An underdeveloped region would be characterized by: 1) a low level of development namely low level of demand (mainly for food products), scarce capital, low saving prospects, and low level of human capital; 2) low level of regional infrastructure, namely weak economic and social infrastructure and low level of local organization; 3) low level of regional status - big economic gaps between regions, regional economic isolation, and insignificant political power. Following the same pattern, middle and high levels of development may be roughly defined.

The classification of levels of development is admittedly quite arbitrary, but we may find some justification for such a ranking. An analysis by Chenery (1982) of several countries at various stages of development indicates that a significant difference exists between countries which are at the middle stage of development and countries at high or low levels of development. Chenery points out that over the past 25 years, there has been a tendency for middle-income countries to grow more rapidly than richer or poorer countries. The explanation proposed for such a phenomenon is based on three elements: 1) a sharp rise in the rate of accumulation of physical capital and skills; 2) a shift of labor and capital into sectors that can use them more efficiently, where demand is increasing more rapidly; and 3) a diversification of the economic structure which makes the economy less vulnerable to changes in trade or demand.

This explanation seems applicable not only in the case of countries, but in the case of regions as well. At the lowest level of development we find very few growth opportunities as a result of start-up difficulties (see Fig. 3). At this level, the possibility of industrializing the region is restricted by lack of infrastructure and capital and by the unskilled labor force, as outlined earlier. Consequently, at this stage the growth rate of industries is very low and, the need for development efforts in order to stimulate industrialization is high. At the second medium level of development, the ability of industry to grow is at its highest: demand increases rapidly, the level of infrastructure is higher, the labor force is better skilled and conditions are mature for rapid industrial growth. Moreover, at this stage the cost invested by the government is highly effective namely less effort is needed than at the previous level. At the third- and highest- stage of development the level of infrastructure is good and the labor force is skilled, but the increase in demand for industrial products is not as rapid as it was at the second stage, because we have reached a relative saturation point of the market. At this level the region attains equilibrium and the need for further industrial development efforts decreases.

INDUSTRIALIZATION AND EXTERNAL CONDITIONS

As explained above, external conditions determine the framework within which the process of industrialization (and its relations with development) takes place. It is roughly assumed that those external conditions can be considered as exogenous variables, meaning that they exert influence on the process of industrialization and

Figure 3. Schematic Illustration of Three Levels of Development

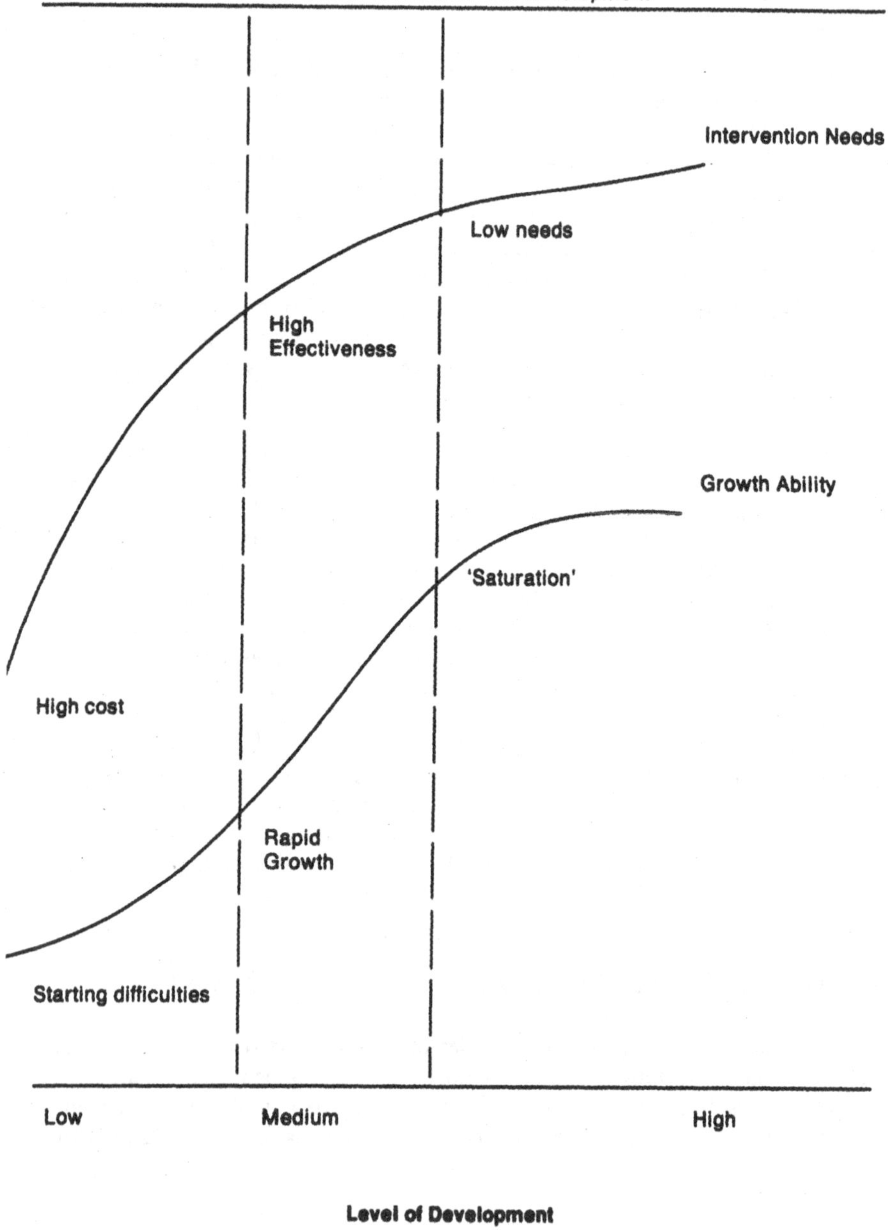

development, but are not necessarily influenced by it. The exogenous variables may be divided into two groups (Fig. 4): variables related to the national development approach, and variables related to the natural economic potential of the region.

Figure 4. Main Components of External Conditions

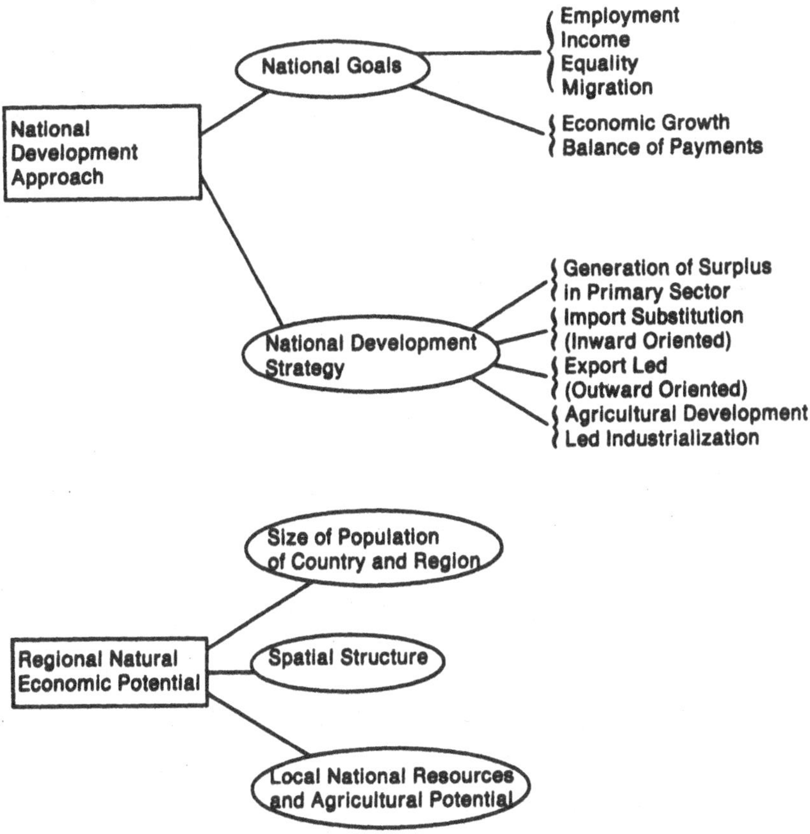

The first group includes two main aspects: the national development goals and the national development strategy which is adopted for the achievement of such goals. The national goals may include raising rates of employment, raising incomes, reducing inequalities between regions, improving quality of life and services, decreasing migration from rural to urban sectors, increasing overall economic growth of the nation (GNP/capita) and improving the balance of payments. Without entering into a detailed analysis, we can say that the goals largely fall into two groups: national economic goals and socio-economic goals. An improvement in the balance of payments or overall economic growth, for example, are economic goals on the national level whereas goals related to employment, income, equality and migration consider not only the economic aspect of development but also some of its social aspects, and its expression in relation to individuals and regions and not only in terms of aggregate national indicators.(16)

It is quite clear that the determination of national goals has direct or indirect implications on the role of the industrial sector, and specifically the types of manufacturing activities which should be stimulated. Creating employment, for example, may be best achieved by certain branches such as textiles or food,(17) while other branches may be more apt to increase income.(18) Size of plants may also influence employment and equality of distribution.(19) 'High-tech' industries may be efficient in promoting national economic growth or increasing income, but not necessarily in increasing employment levels.(20)

Given the national goals, policy makers chose a national development strategy. The variety of development operative strategies may be classified into a few well known categories that have been discussed thoroughly in the literature. The divisions we present here have been shown by Chenery (1982) and Balassa (1980), amongst others. The first policy aims at generating a surplus in the primary sector, beyond the subsistence level. This strategy, which is adopted particularly at low levels of development where subsistence agriculture is the primary source of living, considers the agriculture sector as a vehicle for economic development. The other three strategies refer to the industrial sector. The import substitution strategy is defined by Balassa (1980) as a two-stage process.(21) At the first stage growth of production is faster than growth of consumption, making possible an industrial development based on the substitution of imported consumer goods. When this process comes to an end, import substitution is directed towards the production of intermediary products and capital goods (as opposed to consumption goods at the first stage). Because of its basic structure, the import substitution strategy tends to discriminate against rural industrialization, since in most cases the rural area cannot offer the necessary conditions for that kind of industrial activity.

Outward-oriented policy or export-led growth is a third policy option. Industrialization should not aim at producing goods for domestic consumption, but rather exploit the factors in which the country has a comparative advantage. It should concentrate its activity on the production and exportation of goods based on this comparative advantage and, parallely import products in which the country does not have a comparative advantage.(22) This strategy has also many negative implications regarding the ability of such manufacturing activities to locate in rural areas and to integrate into the local economy.(23)

A fourth strategy has been proposed recently by Adleman (1984), and is denominated as the Agricultural Development Led Industrialization (ADLI). In view of the problems of export-led industrialization resulting from the protectionist policies imposed by developed countries against cheaper foreign imports, Adleman proposes a strategy based on local agriculture development. In this policy industrialization is based not on the comparative advantage relative to other countries, but on local resources. Using a quantitative model for Korea, she illustrates how such an approach can create high economic growth rate and even generate more exports than under export-led growth policy. The main difference, however, is that with ADLI exports are mostly agriculture based goods.

The second group of exogenous variables is the natural economic potential of the region. It consists of three sub-groups of variables representing the ability of the region to provide a basis for industrial development: size of population, spatial structure and the existence of local natural resources or of an agricultural potential.

The size of the population provides a market for industry at its first stage of development and a larger and more varied labor force from which to draw. Many industrial plants which cannot be justified in regions with small populations could be feasible in more populated areas.(24) A second aspect is the spatial pattern of the region, namely the distances between the region and large urban centers, the hierarchy of cities within the region and the position of the region within the hierarchical structure of the nation (if there is such an hierarchical structure). Such a pattern will have significant implications regarding the ability of the industrialization process in the region to integrate into the national economic structure. The third aspect relates to the existence of local natural resources and agricultural potential: a region that has large natural resources or a strong agricultural potential is expected to offer more industrialization opportunities than a region which is less endowed.(25)

A SIMPLIFIED CLASSIFICATION OF EXOGENOUS CONDITIONS

Theoretically there is a large number of exogenous typologies, resulting from all the possible combinations between various possible values of all the relevant variables. We believe, however, that due to internal correlations between variables which define the various aspects of exogenous conditions, the number of actual typologies is much smaller.

It is beyond the scope of this paper to enter into a detailed determination and analysis of all the empirically probable typologies. We shall therefore limit ourselves to a very schematic classification of exogenous conditions, using a rough definition and categorization of variables. According to this technique the national development approach consists of two categories: an economic-oriented approach that maximizes growth of GNP and improves the balance of payments, and a socioeconomic-oriented approach that involves employment, equality, etc. The regional natural economic potential may also be divided into two categories: high potential and low potential.

The four main types would thus be:

Type 1 A region with high natural economic potential in a country which adopts a purely economic development approach.

Type 2 A region with high natural economic potential in a country oriented towards socioeconomic objectives.

Type 3 A region with low natural economic potential in a country with an economic development approach.

Type 4 A region with low economic natural potential in a country with a socioeconomic development approach.

The immediate impression is that the best opportunities for rural industrial development can be found in a region of type 2, and the worst - in a region of type

3 which, by definition is located in a country that focuses its development efforts on stronger regions and urban centers.

A FEW HYPOTHESES ABOUT GROWTH PATTERNS IN REGIONAL INDUSTRIALIZATION

After having defined the general approach showing that regional industrialization is one element within the whole system of dynamic socioeconomic development and external conditions and constraints, and after having defined in broad terms the specific factors which compose each of the three main parts of such a system, we shall now try to state a few general hypotheses regarding the operation of such a system. In general, the hypotheses will relate to the effect of external conditions and the endogenous process of development on growth patterns of regional industrialization. We shall first refer to a few general principles and then formulate more specific hypotheses.

GENERAL PRINCIPLES

At low levels of economic development, we should prefer an industrial policy which has three major characteristics: (1) it aims at solving problems of unemployment rather than raising income and standards of living; (2) it is linked more to the economic development of the region than to the national economic structure (namely uses mainly inputs from agriculture and other local resources and produces output for the local market; (3) it aims at a relatively slow rate of growth which is suitable to the rate of improvement in the local infrastructure and to the increase in demand.

At higher levels of economic development, policy should include industrial strategies which emphasize more the improvement of the standard of living rather than the creation of new jobs, and strive for a higher degree of integration with the national economic structure. Moreover, the policy should encourage faster growth rate, which will be made possible by higher levels of demand and better infrastructure, until it reaches a saturation point.

SPECIFIC RELATIONS BETWEEN THE INDUSTRIAL CHARACTERISTICS AND THE ENDOGENOUS DEVELOPMENT PROCESS

The following hypotheses refers to the simplified classification suggested above into three basic levels of development, and try to specify which industrial characteristics would be most adequate at each stage. The hypotheses are derived from the general considerations presented above, and from existing theoretical and empirical experience.

1. At low levels of development labor-intensive activities should have a priority due to the needs to create employment and because of the scarcity of capital; a shift should be made at higher levels of development towards more capital

intensive activities.(26) In any case, neither extremely labor-intensive nor capital-intensive activities should be adopted.(27)

2. Industrialization should begin with unsophisticated production processes, and shift towards more advanced technologies and better skills at higher levels of development. Such shifts should however be restricted quantitatively in proportion to the share of the labor-force that acquired higher education and skills; and qualitatively - to processes which have less agglomeration needs (most research and development activities would therefore be excluded).

3. At the beginning of the development process, industrial development should be based predominantly on household and small-scale plants as a means for best local integration.(28) As development proceeds, small-scale plants cannot continue to serve as basis for industrialization, and a gradual shift towards medium-scale plants should be considered.(29)

4. At the first stages of development the main industrial production should concentrate on consumer products with a low income elasticity of demand, such as food, some clothing products, etc.; at later stages it should shift to products with higher income elasticity of demand.

5. At first steps local markets should be the focus of industrial production, expanding later to regional, national and perhaps international markets.

6. At low levels of development, most industrial activity should focus on a few products expanding to a larger diversity of products at higher levels of development.(30) A higher level of development would therefore mean the evolution of more advanced plants (more capital-intensive, higher know-how requirements, etc.), but it would not mean a shift in focus from one type of industrial activities to another. A larger diversity, as suggested by this hypothesis, would mean the evolution of an industrial structure involving a wider range of products, technologies and markets. These would fulfill the needs of various groups of the labor-force, with diverse skills and aspirations.

7. At the lowest levels of development backward and forward linkages of manufacturing plants would occur mainly on a local level (with agricultural and local markets); at higher levels they will spread to more spatially dispersed linkages with other markets, other sources of raw materials and industrial plants in other regions.(31)

8. At low levels of development we would also expect more plants the main locational factors of which are the existence of local raw materials, a local market and cheap labor. Such factors would be less significant at more advanced levels of development.

9. At low levels of development, the spatial structure of manufacturing plants would show a pattern of dispersed, small local plants, at higher levels of development a more hierarchical spatial structure will emerge.

RELATIONS BETWEEN INDUSTRIAL CHARACTERISTICS AND EXTERNAL CONDITIONS

In the following we suggest two general hypotheses regarding the effects of external conditions on rural-regional industrialization, derived from the above presentation of the relevant variables.

1. As far as the national approach is concerned, the concentration on pure national economic goals would involve a centralized industrialization process, characterized by high capital-intensity, more advanced technologies and marginal involvement of the rural area.(32) A more socio-economic approach would involve development strategies which are closer to the Agricultural Development Led Industrialization (ADLI) than to import substitution or export-led industrialization. If employment and distribution are predominant objectives for regional development, industrialization will tend to be more traditional, small-scale and locally oriented. As objectives shift towards increasing income levels and improving standards of living, industrialization will be characterized by a higher development level.

2. Favourable conditions in the region or in the country, expressed by bigger size (bigger markets, abundant supply of labor-force), better economic potential (natural resources, good agricultural opportunities) and a balanced spatial structure will help the industrialization process achieve more rapidly the transition from a structure which is most adequate to low levels of development to a structure which is more appropriate to higher levels of development, as described in the previous section.

CONCLUSIONS

The general approach, which is drawn in very broad lines in this paper, can probably be visualised as a set of consecutive questions and directives offered to the industrial planner or policy-maker in a given region, in order to help him decide on the most effective measures under the given conditions. This set of questions may be formulated as follows:

1. What is the national general approach to development in your country? The answer to that question helps determine the quantity and general character of manufacturing activities which can be considered in the region.

2. What is the natural economic potential of your region? The answer to this question will provide important information about plants which can be based on the processing of local resources and potential agricultural products and information about potential demand.

Answers to questions 1 and 2 determine the given framework within which industrial planning has to be made as a result of externally imposed constraints of national approach and economic potential. The following questions intend to provide information on various aspects of development level and characteristics in the region, to be used as input for the determination of optimal industrial measures.

3. What is the level of development of the region in terms of income and demand for industrial products, human capital, and capital accumulation and potential?

4. What are the conditions of the physical infrastructure, the social structure and the organizational patterns in the region?

5. What are the relations between the region and the country in terms of economic gaps, trade relations and political status?

Answers to these questions are expected to help in the elaboration of a plan for industrial development, and in its continuous readjustment with development of the region. In industrial development we do not mean only quantities of manufacturing plants, but also their characteristics. Some of these such characteristics have been enumerated and classified into three main groups: the production process, the product and the spatial patterns of industrial activity.

We have tried to suggest a few hypotheses regarding the operational answers to the above stated questions in terms of industrial characteristics. One of the main points is that at low levels of development, industrial development should strive towards labor-intensive production, small-scale plants, unskilled jobs and local integration. At higher levels of development a shift is proposed to inverse characteristics.

Further research should strive for a more detailed elaboration of the suggested approach, and mainly for a quantitative testing of the hypothesis suggested in the preceding paragraph, so that they can be transformed into operational planning instruments.

NOTES

1. For a definition of high technology in the context of local economic development, see Malecki (1984), pp. 263-4.

2. There are wide variations in the definitions of 'small-scale' industrial activities amongst writers. In broad general terms, this term refers to plants of a size which may be adequate to rural or small local town conditions. See, amongst many others, Molenaar, El-Namaki and Van Dijk (1984); Chuta and Sheturaman (1984); Mazumdar (1984); Page and Steal (1984).

3. See Leechor, Kohli and Hur (1983) for world income elasticities of a few major industrial branches (p. 27).

4. See the interindustry linkage classification presented by Beyers (1981) and based on Chenery and Watanabe, and his linkage typologies using a cluster analysis (pp. 75-85).

5. There are numerous theoretical and empirical works on factors which affect manufacturing location. See a few recent examples which are directly relevant to the issue of regional development: Kale and Lonsdale (1979); Boon (1983); UNIDO (1983); Michel and Ochel (1978); Townroe (1983).

6. A prevailing view, expressed by Boon (1983) and others, is that big capital-intensive industrial plants will remain in urban centers, whereas small industries which employ conventional technologies will prevail in small towns and in rural regions. This is the 'both legs' approach (see especially pp. 56-59).

7. Chenery (1982) defines the transformation of an underdeveloped economy into a developed one by a set of structural changes required to sustain continuity, increase in income and social welfare, and includes in it changes in consumer demand, accumulation of physical and human capital and access to common sources of technology and international demand (p.3).

8. This results from a lower income elasticity of the demand for food products. Chenery (1982) shows this empirically for various countries (see pp. 5, 6, 24).

9. Higher capital-intensity at higher levels of development is achieved not only by the development of new (capital-intensive) activities, but also by increasing capital-intensity at existing type of activities by improving production technologies. See Stern (1977) for an empirical presentation of increasing capital-intensity (decreasing labor-intensity) at various levels of income per capita for given economic sectors (pp. 27-33). See also de Vries and Brakel (1983) for the specific case of textile industry in Pakistan, the Philippines, Portugal and Turkey.

10. Browning (1980) finds that the most important location factor for new products and high technology is the availability of skilled technical and professional manpower.

11. Leechor, Kohli and Hur (1983) present empirical evidence from world industry for the continuing shift towards higher skills and technology and lower degrees of specialization in labor-intensive branches. This is true for developed market economies as well as for less developed countries during the process of development.

12. Malecki (1984) indicates 'quality of life' as one of the most important factors in the location of research and development institutions (pp. 266-7).

13. See Rosenstein-Rodan (1943, 1961) and Datta-Chaudhuri (1982, pp. 237-248) for a detailed discussion of sets of indivisibilities which explain industrial concentration. See also Gwynne (1986) for a detailed analysis of industrial concentration tendencies in Latin America.

14. See, for example, Kale and Lonsdale (1979); Erickson (1976, 1981); Doering and Kinsworthy (1979). Others (such as Storper, 1981) attribute decentralization trends to the changing structure of industrial activity as well.

15. Although the increasing weight of 'hi-technology' industrial activities may have decreased the decentralization trends, Malecki (1981) has found (for the United States) that even this new type of activity already shows first signs of decentralization.

16. An important question, which is not analysed in this paper, is whether there is a conflict or a complementarity between the achievement of the various

goals. For a discussion of this issue, see for example Byerlee, Eicher, Leidhom and Spencer (1983); Jaksch (1974); Morley (1978); Stewart and Streeten (1971); Williams (1981); and Bar-El (1984).

17. See employment multipliers for different branches by Stern (1977), p. 25. Steed (1981) shows that even developed countries protect the clothing industry in order to solve unemployment problems.

18. Michel and Ochel (1978) use a definition of branches by types of linkages and achieve a classification of objectives best achieved by each branch.

19. Small scale plants have more direct and indirect employment effects, as well as more distributional effects (Anderson, 1982).

20. See Jelavich (1984), and Thomas (1981).

21. The 'import-substitution' strategy is the outcome of an analysis of international trade in developing countries by Raul Prebisch (1950). The extensive discussion about that strategy is much beyond the scope of this paper. For a short summary of its limitations see UNIDO (1983) pp. 50-52.

22. See Chenery (1960) and Chenery and Syrquin (1975).

23. See a summary of limitations in UNIDO (1983), pp. 54-56. See also the analysis of difficulties to enter export activities by 'late-starters' such as Kenya, Tanzania and Zambia, by Gulhati and Sekhar (1981), pp. 28-43.

24. This statement is well demonstrated by Chenery (1960, 1982), who shows that a 'big' country can more easily achieve an industrialization process which smaller countries can attain only at higher levels of development.

25. It seems that this argument does not need any literature support. Nevertheless, a few cases are worth mentioning: Johnston and Mellor (1961); Sigurdson (1975); Bacha (1975); Gray (1983).

26. This is consistent with most basic development theories. An analysis made by UNIDO (1983) suggests three consecutive stages: labor-intensive, capital-intensive and science based technology-intensive industrialization. The major relevant manufacturing branches at each stage are indicated: food, textile, clothing and leather at the first; chemicals and others at the second, basic metal, machinery and transportation at the third (see pp. 52-3, 67-71).

27. See Bar-El (1984) for the theoretical support, and for an empirical testing with data from Northeast Brazil, showing that the optimal technology for employment maximization does not involve the adoption of extremely labor-intensive activities. See also Anderson (1982) pp. 58-60.

28. Hakanson (1979) shows that small-scale plants can survive at the early phases of development, since profit margins tend to be wider under conditions of rapidly increasing demand. Such conditions disappear at later stages of development, when the rate of growth in demand tends to decline, competition tends to increase, and economies of scale are more important.

29. Anderson (1982) offers a detailed analysis of three types of industrial plants as classified by scale, and of the relative importance of each type at various stages of development. The three types are: household manufacturing, small workshops and factories, and large-scale plants (pp. 6-27).

30. Lever (1979) shows empirically for Great Britain that 'dominated labor markets' as defined by the predominance of few plants, characterise depressed regions and are less economically stable (pp. 98-103). Havrylyshyn and Civan (1983) prove statistically that the level of development, as measured by per capita income, is the most important predicator of intra-industry trade between countries, resulting from a diversified demand and a greater ability to produce heterogenous products. Leechor, Kohli and Hur (1983) show similar trends in the analysis of world manufacturing trends.

31. See Beyers (1981) for a classification of activities by characteristics of spatial linkage (pp. 75-85).

32. It seems that such an hypothesis does not need anymore any empirical testing. A recent meeting of OEA (1985) reached the conclusion that regional development should be reinforced, since it was weakened by the adoption of 'adjustment' policies in many Latin American countries.

REFERENCES

Adleman, I. "Beyond Export-Led Growth." *World Development* 12:9(1984): 937-949.

Anderson, D. "Small Industry in Developing Countries." *World Bank Staff Working Papers*, No. 518, 1982.

Bacha, E.L. "Industrialization and the Agricultural Sector." *Development Discussion Papers*, Harvard Institute for International Development University, No. 33, 1977.

Balassa, B. "The Process of Industrial Development and Alternative Development Strategies." *World Bank Staff Working Papers*, No. 438, 1980.

Bar-El, R. "Industrialization Objectives: The Income-Employment Conflict." *World Development* 12 (1984): 129-140.

Beyers, W. "Alternative Spatial Linkage Structures in Multi-Regional Economic Systems." In *Industrial Location and Regional Systems*, edited by J. Rees, G. Hewings and H. Stafford. New York: J.F. Bergen Publishers, 1981.

Boon, C.K. "Dualism and Technological Harmony for Balanced Development." *Industry and Development*, UNIDO, No. 9 (1983): 51-73.

Browning, J.E. *How to Select a Business Site*. New York: McGraw-Hill, 1980.

Byerlee, D., Eicher, C.K., Leidholm, D. and Spencer, D.S.C. "Employment-Output Conflicts, Factor Price Distortions, and Choice of Technique: Empirical Results from Sierra Leone." *Economic Development and Cultural Change* 31:2 (1983): 315-336.

Chenery, H.B. "Patterns of Industrial Growth." *American Economic Review* 2 (September 1980).

--------. "Industrialization and Growth." *World Bank Staff Working Papers*, No. 539, 1982.

--------, and Syrquin, M. *Patterns of Development 1950-1970*. London: Oxford University Press, 1975.

Chuta, E., and Sethuraman, S.V., eds. *Rural Small-Scale Industries and Employment in Africa and Asia*. Geneva: International Labour Organization, 1984.

Datta-Chaudhuri, M. "Infrastructure and Location." In *Policies for Industrial Progress in Developing Countries*, edited by J. Cody, H. Hugues, and D. Wall. London: Oxford University Press, 1982.

Doering, T.R., and Kinworthy, J.C. "The Community Satisfactions of Non-Metropolitan Manufacturers." In *Nonmetropolitan Industrialization*, edited by R.E. Lonsdale and H.L. Seyler. New York: John Wiley and Sons, 1979.

Erickson, R.A. "The 'Filtering-Down' Process: Industrial Location in a Nonmetropolitan Area." *Professional Geography* 28 (1976): 54-66.

--------. "Corporations, Branch Plants and Employment Stability in Nonmetropolitan Areas." In *Industrial Location and Regional Systems*, edited by J. Rees, G. Hewings, H. Stafford. New York: J.F. Bergen Publishers, 1981.

Gray, J. "How the Chinese Channel Rural Industry's Profits into Agriculture." *Ceres, FAO* 16(1983): 20-27.

Genlhati, R. and Sekhar, V. "Industrial Strategy for Late Starters: The Experience of Kenya, Tanzania and Zambia." *World Bank Staff Working Paper* No. 457, 1981.

Gwynne, R.N. *Industrialization and Urbanization in Latin America*. Baltimore: The John Hopkins University Press, 1986.

Hakanson, L. "Towards a Theory of Location and Corporate Growth." In *Spatial Analysis, Industry and the Industrial Environment Vol. I*, edited by F.E. Ian Hamilton and G.J.R. Linge. New York: John Wiley and Sons, 1979.

Havrylyshyn, O. and Civan, E. "Intra-Industry Trade and the Stage of Development - A Regression Analysis of Industrial and Developing Countries." In *Intra Industry Trade-Empirical and Methodological Aspects*, edited by P.K.M. Tharakan, Elsevier Science Publishers B.V. (North-Holland), 1983.

Jaksch, H.J. "Income Distribution as an Objective in Development Planning." *De Economist* 122:1 (1974): 122:1 (1974): 1-22.

Jelavich, M.S. "Economic Impact of Potential New Industries in a Four-State Area." *The Annals of Regional Science* 18:1(1984):77-80.

Johnston, B.F., and Mellor, J.W. "The Role of Agriculture in Economic Development." *American Economic Review* (1961):571-81.

Kale, S.R., and Lonsdale, R.E. "Factors Encouraging and Discouraging Plant Location in Nonmetropolitan Areas." In *Nonmetropolitan Industrialization*, edited by R.E. Lonsdale and H.L. Seyler. New York: John Wiley and Sons, 1979.

Leechor, C., Kohli, H., and Hur, S. *Structural Changes in World Industry*. World Bank: Industry and Finance Series, 1983.

Lever, W.F. "Industry and Labor Markets in Great Britain." In *Spatial Analysis, Industry and the Industrial Environment Vol. I*, edited by F.E. Ian Hamilton and G.J.R. Linge. New York: John Wiley and Sons, 1979.

Malecki, E. "Recent Trends in the Location of Industrial Research and Development: Regional Development Implications for the United States." In *Industrial Location and Regional Systems*, edited by J. Rees, G. Hewings, H. Stafford. New York: J.F. Bergen Publishers, 1981.

--------. "High Technology and Local Economic Development." *Journal of the American Planning Association* 50:30(1984):263-269.

Mazumdar, D. "The Issue of Small versus Large in the Indian Textile Industry." *World Bank Staff Working Papers*, No. 645, 1984.

Michel, H., and Ochel, W. "Rural Industrialisation in Developing Countries." *Economics* (Tuebingen) 18(1978):42-76.

Molenaar, N., El-Namaki, M., and van Rijk, M., eds. *Small Scale Industry Promotion in Developing Countries*. Netherlands: Research Institute for Management Science, 1983.

Morley, S.A. "Mudan&cced.as no Emprego e na Distribu&cced.&atil.o da Renda Durante o 'Milagre Brasileiro'." *Pesqisa e Planejamento Econômico* 8:2(1978):331-366.

OEA. *Report of the Technical Seminar on Regional Development, April 22-24, 1985, Buenos Aires, Argentina*, 1985 (mimeo).

Page, J. and Steel, W. "Small Enterprise Development." *World Bank Technical Paper*, Industry and Finance Series, 1984.

Rosenstein-Rodan, P.N. "Problems of Industrialization of Eastern and South-Eastern Europe." *Economic Journal* (1943):202-11

--------. "Notes on the Theory of the 'Big Push'." In *Economic Development for Latin America*, edited by H.S. Ellis. New York: St. Martins Press, 1961.

Sigurdson, J. "Rural Industrialization in China: Approaches and Results." *World Development* 3,7,8(1975):527-538.

Steed, G. "International Location and Comparative Advantage: The Clothing Industries and Developing Countries." In *Spatial Analysis, Industry and the Industrial Environment Vol. II*, edited by F.E.I. Hamilton and G.J.R. Linge. New York: John Wiley & Sons, 1981.

Stern, J. "The Employment Impact of Industrial Investment: A Preliminary Report." *World Bank Staff Working Paper*, No. 255, 1977.

Stewart, F. and Streeten, P. "Conflicts Between Output and Employment Objectives in Developing Countries." *Oxford Economic Papers* 23, (1971):145-168.

Storper, M. "Toward a Structural Theory of Industrial Location." In *Industrial Location and Regional Systems*, edited by J. Rees, G. Hewings and H. Stafford. New York: J.F. Bergen Publishers, 1981.

Thomas, M. "Industry Perspectives on Growth and Change in the Manufacturing Sector." In *Industrial Location and Regional Systems*, edited by J. Rees, G. Hewings and H. Stafford. New York: J.F. Bergen Publishers, 1981.

Townroe, P. "Location Factors in the Decentralization of Industry." *World Bank Staff Working Paper*, No. 517, 1983.

UNIDO. "The Poor Fall Behind on Assessment of Industry in the Least Developed Countries." *Industry and Development* 8(1983):17-44.

UNIDO. "A Strategy of Industrial Development for the Small, Resource-Poor, Least Developed Countries." *Industry and Development*, 8(1983):45-72.

de Vries, B. and Brakel, W. "Restructuring and Manufacturing Industry". In *The Experience of the Textile Industry in Pakistan, Philippines, Portugal and Turkey, World Bank Staff Working Papers*, No. 558, 1983.

Williams, D.G. "Objective Function Trade Off Curves in a Rural Economic Development Activity Analysis Model." *The Annals of Regional Science* 15:3 (1981):55-72.

THE GOVERNMENT ROLE IN PRIVATE INVESTMENT

Dafna Schwartz*

BACKGROUND

In many countries economic development and social conditions are uneven between regions. The historical reasons for the emergence of such gaps vary from one country to another. In some cases certain regions have suffered absolute economic decline, while in other cases regions have stagnated at a time when most of the country enjoyed economic prosperity. Despite the variety of reasons for underdevelopment in certain areas, we can find similar features and draw some common conclusions. Most of the regions which we consider less developed have a higher level of unemployment or underemployment and less satisfactory social and environmental conditions. Generally speaking, the standard of living in such areas is lower than in other parts of the country. Since many of these so-called disparities are of a degree which is regarded in the countries concerned as unacceptable, governments try to intervene in the open market with a policy aimed at raising the level of economic activity in those regions and at changing its character. This policy is characterized by one of the following strategies or a combination of several:

1. Improving the physical infrastructure and the business environment in the region. A government might improve the roads, the telephone system and the financial and business services.

*The author wishes to thank Mr. Dan Spiegel for his comments and editorial assistance.

2. Establishing a support system for industries in the area. This may include government-sponsored training courses, managerial advice, financial and technical consulting.

3. A system of direct financial incentives designed for entrepreneurs who invest in the region, such as tax abatement programmes, loans, etc.

4. Incentives for the local population such as rent subsidies, housing grants, reduced income tax for local residents and so on.

5. Raising the quality of life in the region by creating public parks and building cultural and athletic facilities.

The third strategy, direct financial incentives, is the key instrument used to solve the problems of development inequality in both the economic and social spheres. I shall therefore concentrate on this point. Whether regional development plans involve grants for equipment or buildings, subsidized or guaranteed loans, fiscal concessions given on investment. profits or taxes, or the improvement of local infrastructure, the aim of all incentives is to help reduce the additional costs of investment in disadvantaged zones. But as we shall see, lower investment costs are not the main criteria for the investing firm and some studies indicate that while much lip service is paid by the business sector and by governments regarding the importance of reducing tax rates and other financial incentives in attracting new investment, in reality these fiscal benefits play only a small role in the decision making process (Howland, 1985; Harrison and Kanter, 1978).(1)

DIRECT INCENTIVES

What are direct incentives? Within the context of regional development direct financial incentives can be defined as those financial benefits which are given to a firm investing in a designated region. In order to close economic gaps, through fiscal incentives governments try to increase the level and often to change the type of industrial investment in less developed regions. The incentives are required because in such regions investment that is profitable for society as a whole may be unprofitable for individual entrepreneurs under the circumstances. Appropriately designed incentives can narrow the gap between public and private returns and induce entrepreneurs to undertake the investments (Galenson, 1984; Little, 1974).

The various forms of aid which are available in the regions selected for development are presented in Table 1. Direct financial incentives fall largely into three categories: capital grants, interest related subsidies and tax concessions. One should bear in mind that all the listed incentives offered to investors benefit the firm in the short-term; the firm receives help only during the first years after initial investment. In order to evaluate the impact of the level and type of the incentives on regional investment we have to examine the way in which entrepreneurs(2) perceive and act upon such incentives (Fig. 1).

Figure 1. Perspective of the Entrepreneur (Economic Feasibility)

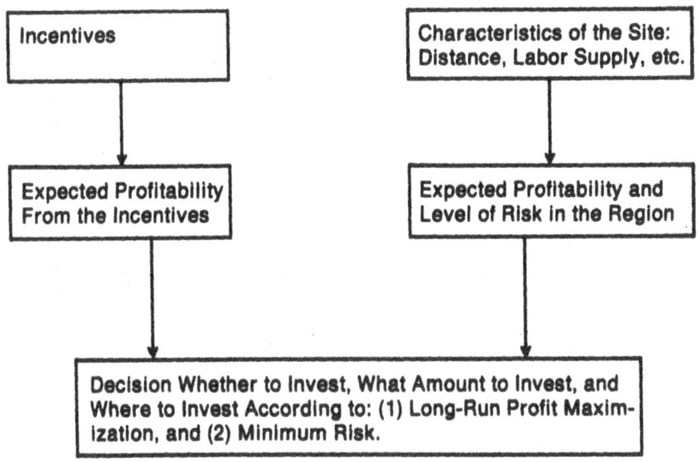

Our primary assumption is that a firm decides whether to invest, what amount to invest and where to invest according to an economic calculation. The goals are profit maximization in the long-term and minimum risk, goals which may compete one against the other. The investment decision of a multi-plant firm makes is based on the profitability of all the branches, while investment decision of a firm which has only one branch is based on the profitability of the single investment. In each of the potential locations the firm considers on the one hand, the specific characteristics of the region, and on the other hand, the potential benefits the government might offer. With these factors in mind, the firm makes the appropriate net calculation and then makes the investment decision - whether to invest, what amount and where. Let us consider for a moment the type of investment which would be made in the designated regions without government intervention.

NON-INTERVENTION SCENARIO

As already stated, a firm decides to invest according to an economic calculation. In each location, the firm weighs the pluses and minuses of the site, and makes a calculation of what effect the site's characteristics will have on their expected profitability. The key factors or characteristics which a firm considers (Armine, 1975; Czamanski, 1981a, 1981b; Isard, 1956) are:

Distance. A site far from raw materials, from the business center of the country, or from the target markets necessarily increases the cost of production.

Table 1: Forms of Aid Available in the Regions Selected for Development

Forms of aid	Yes	No	N.A.	Australia	Austria	Belgium	Canada	Denmark	Finland	France	Germany (FRG)	Ireland	Italy	Japan	Norway	Nether-lands	Spain	Sweden	Turkey	United Kingdom	United States
Investment grants for:																					
machinery and equipment	13	5	—	N	Y	Y	Y	Y	Y	Y	Y	Y	Y	N	Y	Y	Y	N	N	Y	N
industrial buildings	14	4	—	N	Y	Y	Y	Y	Y	Y	Y	Y	Y	N	Y	Y	Y	Y	N	Y	N
Factory buildings	10	8	—	Y	Y	N	N	Y	Y	Y	N	Y	Y	N	Y	N	N	Y	N	Y	N
Industrial land and sites	12	6	—	Y	Y	Y	N	N	N	Y	Y	Y	Y	Y	Y	N	Y	N	Y	Y	N
Loans:																					
at market rate	9	9	—	Y	N	N	N	N	Y	Y	N	Y	N	Y	Y	N	N	Y	Y	Y	N
at subsidized rate	14	4	—	Y	Y	Y	N	Y	N	Y	Y	N	Y	Y	N	Y	Y	Y	Y	Y	Y
guaranteed	15	3	—	Y	Y	Y	Y	N	Y	Y	Y	Y	Y	N	Y	Y	Y	Y	N	Y	Y
Fiscal concessions:																					
on investment	11	7	—	N	N	Y	Y	N	Y	Y	Y	Y	Y	N	Y	Y	Y	N	Y	N	N
on profits	6	12	—	N	N	Y	N	N	Y	N	Y	Y	Y	N	Y	N	N	N	N	N	N
on investment aid received from State	7	11	—	N	Y	Y	N	N	N	Y	Y	N	Y	N	Y	N	N	N	N	Y	N
on State charges, local taxes, licence fees, etc.	12	6	—	Y	Y	Y	N	N	Y	Y	N	Y	Y	Y	Y	N	Y	N	Y	Y	N
Grants towards labour costs	5	13	—	N	Y	N	Y	N	Y	N	N	N	N	N	N	N	N	Y	N	Y	N
Grants towards employment costs, i.e., social security costs	3	15	—	N	Y	N	N	N	Y	N	N	N	Y	N	N	N	N	N	N	N	N
Assistance towards operating costs	3	15	—	N	N	N	N	N	N	N	N	N	Y	N	N	N	N	N	N	Y	Y
Assistance towards moving and settling-in costs of the firm	10	8	—	Y	N	Y	N	Y	N	Y	N	N	Y	Y	Y	Y	N	Y	N	Y	N
Aids for manpower mobility and re-location	13	5	—	Y	Y	Y	N	Y	Y	Y	N	Y	Y	Y	Y	Y	N	Y	N	Y	N
State shareholding	9	9	—	N	N	Y	N	N	Y	N	N	Y	Y	N	Y	Y	Y	N	Y	Y	N
Transport and other public service concessions	6	12	—	Y	N	N	N	N	Y	N	Y	N	N	N	Y	N	N	Y	Y	N	N
Preferential treatment in the award of Government contracts	8	9	1	Y	Y	N	N	N	N	N.A.	Y	N	Y	N	Y	N	N	Y	Y	Y	N
Manpower training aids	13	4	1	Y	Y	Y	N	Y	Y	Y	N	Y	N.A.	Y	Y	Y	Y	Y	N	Y	N
Other	6	6	6	N.A.	N.A.	N	N	N.A.	Y	N.A.	N	N	N	N.A.	N.A.	Y	Y	Y	N	Y	Y

Y = Yes; N = No; N.A. = Not applicable.

Source: Reproduction from Report on *The Role of Industrial Incentives in Regional Development*, p. 16. OECD, Paris, 1979.

Availability of Labor Force. Firms which need unskilled labor naturally prefer to locate in a region where such workers are most plentiful, while firms which need skilled laborers seek a region where a large number of such workers is available. This is the most important factor which a firm weighs when making a location decision.

Level of Physical Infrastructure and Business Services. Good telecommunication services, road networks and readily available business services are important considerations for the investing firm.

The Existence of Other Plants in the Region and Specifically Other Plants in a Similar Industrial Branch. The existence of industries which are already operating in the region is an attractive sign to incoming firms both practically and psychologically. If other industries are found in the region, a minimum level of industrial services most likely exists as well. Furthermore, there is something reassuring to a new investor who sees other enterprises successfully operating in the region.

Availability and Cost of Land and Industrial Buildings. Available industrial sites at a reasonable price makes it easier for a new firm to enter the region.

Image of the Region. The better the image of the region, the lower the perceived risk to the investor.

Quality of Life. Quality social and cultural facilities which would benefit potential employees are an added feature which firms look for when making a location decision.

WHICH FIRMS INVEST IN THE REGION WITHOUT THE INCENTIVES?

Without the incentives the firm's investment decision in a region is a function of the above listed criteria. Which factors are most important in location decision making naturally depend on the type of firm which is seeking to invest. All firms, however, invest according to long-run profit maximization. Without government incentives the only firms which would invest in a development area are those which can make a long-run profit in the region and make use of the region's relative advantage. Nevertheless, the more important question is which firms will *not* invest in the region, and these can be divided into four groups:

1. Firms which lack know-how and capital.

2. Firms which have know-how but lack capital.

3. Firms which have both know-how and capital, but incur additional short-run costs in the region.

4. Firms which find a permanent disadvantage in the region, with the exception of firms which come to exploit the benefits and firms which lack information.

In the first group we have firms that lack technical knowledge, business know-how, capital, etc. Such firms may have the initiative to start a plant, but the potential entrepreneurs may not know, for example, which machinery is best or how to obtain government assistance, and may not be able to obtain financing. These firms, mostly small-scale industries, need more than capital and require a significant learning period.

In the second group there are firms which might have the knowledge, but find it difficult to receive start-up capital in the open market. The less known the entrepreneur, the riskier the investment or the less suitable, the more difficult will it be for him to obtain capital in the open market.

In the third group we have firms which may have both the know-how and capital, yet face an additional short-run cost which discourages the investment in the region. The entrepreneur may be willing to invest, but he may not have the capital to relocate his plant, prepare a site or build a new facility.

In the fourth group we have the firm which must necessarily incur permanent additional costs if it were to invest in the development region. Alone in the free market, this type of firm would invest only in a region which has characteristics that give the firm a relative advantage.

FIRMS AND INCENTIVES

If we look at the four types of firms just outlined, we can describe the following relationship between incentives and industry.

1. For the first firm, which lacks both know-how and capital, direct financial incentives are not an effective solution.

2. For the second firm, which has the know-how but lacks capital in the short-run, direct financial incentives can be of some assistance in the short-run, but they may have some side-effects which are counter to the policy makers' objectives. Since the incentives are available to entrepreneurs who find it difficult to obtain financing in the open market, the aid encourages risky investment. Furthermore, incentives are granted only during the establishment stage, and do not continue long enough to allow the firm which has financial difficulties to "stand up on its feet."

3. For the third firm, which has both know-how and financial resources, the financial incentives can be helpful, but might encourage capital intensive production. For example, in Israel in 1978 capital per worker in development regions was 35 percent higher than in other regions of the country (Ministry of Industry and Commerce, 1981).

4. For the fourth firm, which finds a permanent disadvantage in the region, the incentives are not enough to attract new investment. Short-term financial compensation will not tempt this firm to change its location and invest in

government-designated areas. Take the example of a high-tech firm which requires a skilled work force. Such a firm is not capable of setting up a plant in a region where the labor supply is generally unskilled and little educated, regardless of the direct financial incentives offered. We do, however, find two exceptional cases.

The first exception is a firm which has operations in several locations. It may establish a branch in a development area only to receive the benefits from the government and use these benefits to better its financial position or to improve the public stature of the firm. Toren (1979), for example, has shown that some large Israeli industrial concerns established plants in development towns in the 1960's not because the investment was profitable by itself, but rather to receive financial benefits or government favouritism for their other operations.

Another exception is the case of the firm which invests in the region by mistake. The firm may have lacked full information when it made its investment decision, or it may have made a poor business calculation. In any case, 'easy' government money can encourage a firm to mistakenly invest in the region. In either case the scenario is clear: these firms cannot be profitable in the region. If they do come, they will inevitably have to close the plant or relocate to another area.

CONCLUSIONS

If we look back on all the cases, we may conclude that direct financial incentives are only partially effective at best, and can be a source of instability in the development regions. We find firms which come and go causing overall instability and uncertainty in a region which is already handicapped. In a study of the impact of property tax incentives on intra-regional location of new firms, it was concluded that neither property tax rates nor the existence of tax abatement programme influenced new firm births or locations in four Atlantic states (Howland, 1985). Similar conclusions were drawn in a study of firms in the city of Detroit (Wolkoff, 1984). Take the example of Ofakim, a development town of about 13,000 residents in the Negev region of Israel. In a study of Ofakim (Bar-El and Schwartz, 1985), we found that 70 percent of the plants which came and started operations between the years 1971 and 1981 had closed down and left by 1983. Furthermore, we also found that there was no change in the type of industry that located in the town during those ten years. Both theoretical and empirical research indicate that there is no reason to expect that tax or related cost-side incentives will by themselves generate new investment which otherwise would not have been taken (Harrison and Kanter, 1978).

RECOMMENDATIONS

In order to improve the incentive system and avoid economic distortions, policy makers must consider the following points:

1. In order to encourage small-scale industries, which according to the literature are most beneficial to less developed regions, policy should be aimed at creat-

ing some sort of 'supporting system' for small-scale entrepreneurs, such as government sponsored training courses, managerial advice, financial and technical consulting (Rondinelli, 1979).

2. Incentives must act directly upon the problem or disadvantage. They should not be blanket grants or tax breaks which are apt to be used by firms that do not need them, thus taking away potential income from the government and not encouraging new economic growth. Subsidies should be specifically offered for plant relocation, for preparing industrial sites or for worker training programmes.

3. Incentives such as tax breaks and low-cost financing should remain in effect both during the establishment stage and during the early operational years and then decrease gradually.

4. Subsidies must be given to labor as well in order to offset the imbalance of relative prices between capital and labor created by financial incentives. Grants and loans encourage capital intensive investments, when often the actual goal of regional industrialization is the creation of new job opportunities. Labor subsidies, such as a reduction in income tax, should be offered to encourage the competitive use of labor.

5. If the goal of the policy makers is to change the type of industry in a region, away from the traditional branches of textiles and food products for example, financial incentives alone are not enough. The fundamental structure of the region needs to be altered, and this can only be accomplished by employing a combination of the various financial and non-financial incentives outlined earlier.

Any government regional development policy must include some combination of all the strategies, both financial and non-financial. What the specific weight of each strategy will be is a function of the level of development in the region relative to other regions; the lower the level of development, the more important the non-financial strategies. Only a concerted, intensive effort on the part of governments using all the strategies outlined will allow underdeveloped regions to break away from their inferior position.

NOTES

1. For a parallel discussion of the subject of fiscal incentives and their impact on foreign investment see Lim, 1980.

2. In the context of this paper the term entrepreneur refers to individuals within the firm who are responsible for making investment decisions.

REFERENCES

Armine, H., Ritchey, Y. and Hulley,O. *Manufacturing Organization and Management*. Englewood Cliffs: Prentice Hall, 1975.

Bar-El, R. and Schwartz, D. *Economic Development of Ofakim: A Few Preliminary Considerations.* Working Paper Series 14. Rehovot: Settlement Study Centre, 1986.

Chen-Young, P. "A Study of Tax Incentives in Jamaica." *National Tax Journal* 20:3 (1967): 292-308.

Cody, J., Hughes, H. and Wall, D. (eds.) *Policies for Industrial Progress in Developing Countries.* New York: Oxford University Press, 1980.

Czamanski, D. "A Contribution to the Study of Industrial Location Decisions." *Environmental Planning* 13 (1981): 29-42.

--------. "Some Considerations Concerning Industrial Location Decisions." *European Journal of Operational Research* 6:2 (1981): 227-231.

Galenson, A. *Investment Incentives for Industry: Some Guidelines for Developing Countries.* World Bank Staff Working Papers No. 669, 1984.

Harrison, B., and Kanter, S. "The Political Economy of States: Job-Creation Business Incentives." *Journal of the American Planning Association* (October 1978): 424-435.

Isard, W. *Location and Space Economy.* Cambridge: MIT Press, 1956.

Lim, D. "Fiscal Incentives and Direct Foreign Investment in LDC's." *Journal of Development Studies* (1982): 207-211.

--------. "Taxation Policies." In *Policies for Industrial Progress in Developing Countries*, edited by J. Cody, H. Hughes and D. Wall. New York: Oxford University Press, 1980.

Little, I. and Mirrlees, T. *Project Appraisal and Planning for Developing Countries.* London: Heinemann Educational Books, 1974.

McGreevy, T., and Thomson, A. "Regional Policy and Company Investment Behaviour." *Regional Studies* XVII:5 (1983): 347-357.

Meyer-Krahmer, F.G.G., and Kuntze, U. "Impacts of Government Incentives Towards Industrial Innovation." *Research Policy*, 12:3 (June 1983): 153-169.

Ministry of Industry and Commerce. "Objectives for the Development of Industry in Israel, 1978-1980." Jerusalem: Centre for Industrial Planning, 1980.

OECD. *Report on the Role of Industrial Incentives in Regional Development.* Paris, 1979.

Rondinelli, D. "Small Industries in Rural Development: Assessment and Perspective." *Productivity News* XVI:12 (February 1979): 19-33.

Schwartz, D. "The Effective Incentive Involved in the Law for Encouraging Capital Investment." *The Economic Quarterly* 31:124 (March 1985): 12-21 (Hebrew).

Toren, B. *The Inducement Subsidy for Location of Textile Mills in Development Towns in Israel (1958-1965).* Ph.D. Dissertation, Hebrew University of Jerusalem, 1979 (Hebrew).

Wolkoff, M. "Chasing a Dream: The Use of Tax Abatements to Spur Urban Economic Development." *Urban Studies* 22 (1985): 305-315.

Part 5: Organizational Factors in Rural Regional Development

THE NEGOTIATED ORDER APPROACH TO REGIONAL DEVELOPMENT

Julia Margulies

INTRODUCTION

When approaching a single region, development planners find it difficult to elaborate a strategy which is both change-oriented and politically feasible. Most developing regions even in different countries, have in common the basic problem that their development is determined by economic and institutional environments which are not supportive enough. Normative planning, that assumes optimal norms of behaviour both in the region and in the nation, proved to be ineffective. The present paper raises the issue of reconciling strategies to the fact that the development of a given region is the outcome of its negotiation power vis-a-vis the national centre. The circumstances of many Latin American rural regions can provide such an example.

NATIONAL FACTORS AFFECTING REGIONAL DEVELOPMENT

Three factors at the national level are especially important when dealing with regional development: the country's overall economic background, its development policies and priorities and the patterns of implementation as these are indicators of the will and determination as well as the capability of inducing change. Until recently, the economy of Latin American countries had been based historically, mainly on the primary sector (agriculture and mining). In the agriculture sector, and in rural regions in general, two distinct sub-sectors emerged, creating an effective socioeconomic dualism: export on one hand and subsistence on the other, with the latter connected only partially, or not at all, with the market. Consequently, estate and mine owners and urban merchants controlling large economic resources became the ruling political coalition (Barraclough, 1971; Feder, 1972).

The one-sided dependence on the export of primary products made the economy of these countries highly vulnerable to ecological and market conditions. This situation culminated during the world economic crisis of the thirties, which brought about a sharp decline in exports and falling prices. That period proved very difficult for the ruling elites and their policies which were molded to suit particularly the export interests. In later periods, and particularly following the Second World War, a search was on for a new development model (Garcia, 1973). The solution which emerged supported industrialization as a means for broadening exports and limiting imports, thus reducing the dependence on foreign countries. At the same time, the previous political balance was upset as emergent urban groups strove to influence development policy and benefit from its rewards. All in all, industrialization has come to be considered as the dynamic vehicle for growth and modernization, with consumer demands for goods and services influencing its scope and composition. However as industrialization concentrated in urban metropolitan areas, its effects intensified the intersectoral gaps.(1)

It was in the course of the implementation of this type of development that national governments assumed a more active role. While earlier they had been primarily concerned with security, foreign policy, representation and mediation between the various groups and interests of the ruling elite, they now became concerned also with planning and with the creation of physical and institutional infrastructure for both production and marketing. At the national level, Bolivia, Colombia and Chile were the first countries to formulate development plans. Since the conference at Punta del Este in 1961 (Naciones Unidas, 1970), all the Latin American countries have prepared development plans of varying scopes and characteristics, however, they all have in common a declarative rather than operational basis. An analysis of national plans indicates that "they led for a wide scope for interpretation, as no indications are made as to priorities, interrelationships and solution of potential conflicts" (Schreider, 1975).

Awareness to the need for national development planning led to the establishment of planning institutions and to the development of bureaucratic structures which became a major source of employment, but these again were primarily urban-based.

In fact, the new development orientations and the expansion of the government role did not change basically the historical dualism in terms of level of development. The rural sector is regarded first and foremost as a source for national accumulation of capital (Lefeber, 1981). The concern with increased production is thus primarily to serve both export, and growing urban demands. This is reflected clearly in the differential support given to the various sectors, to regions, and to sub-sectors within single regions (Rofman, 1982). This fundamental continuity of imbalanced development has hardly been affected by changes, some of them far-reaching, that were introduced in parts of the agrarian system(2) or by shifts to more radical regimes.(3) Nor has it changed through internationalization of capital contrary to some expectations.(4)

That development leads to what Pinto called "the triple concentration of the results of technical progress" (de Mattos, 1981) at the social, e economic and spatial spheres. The result being a further marginalization of the rural regions.

This situation constitutes a basic constraint in the formulation of development goals and strategies in specific regions; and planning institutions find it difficult to elaborate rural regional development plans that are compatible with long-term national policies.

Regarding the capability of implementing regional plans and activating mechanisms for vertical and horizontal integration, the picture is not better. An overall picture of limited capability emerges, which is due to overcentralization, lack of coordination and organizational as well as staff instability, which are derived in most cases from the national level. The major regional agencies are invariably extensions of central governmental departments, and are designed first and foremost, to carry out handed down policies. Similarly, budget allocations reach the region separately through the different ministerial channels, and are earmarked and administered independently.

Moreover, since there is no integral long-range socioeconomic policy which can be translated into an overall set of priorities, clear objectives, or criteria, each ministry designs its policy and chooses its own targets. This practice causes both overlapping - when different ministries attend to the same groups or targets, and lack of action - when no agency feels committed to a certain group or target. The lack of a consistent and detailed development approach leads to over-recurrence to ad hoc solutions, to unsound experiments and to the adoption of immediate measures lacking in time perspective. Organizations and agencies are thus created on the basis of immediate and specific needs or orientations and have a short life span.

This problem is further aggravated by the high turnover of personnel, in national and regional offices, which inevitably creates inexperience and feelings of insecurity among employees.(5) Indeed, there are no clear civil service criteria for transfer of employees, they mostly originate in personal decisions at various administrative levels. As arbitrary creation and elimination of positions is an accepted mechanism of placement, under such conditions, the importance of patronage clearly outweighs professional considerations and evaluation of actual qualifications and performance. In some countries attempts have been made to change this situation by means of decentralization, (Kuitenbrower, 1973; Hilhorst, 1980). Regional agencies with authority, budget and trained professional staff were initiated. But even then, new political regimes had no difficulty in reversing the new trends.

PLANNING THE REGIONAL DEVELOPMENT

On the whole, regional developmental planning is conducted under conditions of uncertainty, and even of anomie, primarily in the sense that there is no consistent, long-range development policy, orientation and infrastructure. Even when there seems to be a commitment to regional development, it has limitations of its own. There have been cases in which initial support for the development of a region was provided, but it proved to be rather short-term and the development efforts were interrupted before changes could take place or before the local population was able to cope with the regional problems by itself.

Given this situation, one possible conclusion would be that planning is irrelevant in that kind of national environment. But on the other hand, there is a strong need to approach problems in a rational and systematic way. The relevant issue seems therefore to be the selection of an adequate strategy to change. Since the institutional 'climate' in which the regional planner has to function is highly unstable, there seems to be little point in what may be called 'normative planning'. 'Normative planning' assumes optimal norms of behaviour, both regional and national, and on this premise puts forward economically optimal goals. What we need instead is a strategy that explicitly focuses on and treats the relations between the focal region and its environment. It is important therefore, that the exact status of the region in this relationship be defined. Most of the items that are objects of transactions between the region and the environment fall into the category of scarce resources and are now, as in the past, a focus of competition between regions. This competition is a continuous process underlying the emergence of the hierarchy of regions in the country. Such an hierarchy seems to be a suitable criterion for the assessment of the situation in a single region. It reflects what may be called the bargaining position of the single region in relation to resources and in relation to competing regions that share its environment.

The consideration of the status of any single region as the outcome of some form of negotiation has further implications. It means that any strategy to develop the region should include a clear reference to the revision of the formerly negotiated order. But at the same time the planner should be aware of what can and what cannot be changed by intervention at the regional level. Not all negotiations are feasible; some actors in the bargaining situation have structurally more power and greater control than others. Therefore, an assessment has to be made of the real possibilities of the focal region to improve its bargaining position through the utilization of its internal resources. This is of particular importance for although social and economic structures in developing regions may be the main obstacles to their development, regions with similar structural features may differ in their potential capabilities to increase their bargaining position and in their consequent differential capabilities to develop under existing constraints.(6) The differential potential of regions to initiate a process of linkage or maintain it can be attributed to several factors. One is the differential status or relative national importance in terms of possessing a national asset or being long-term national assets themselves. Border areas and regions of geopolitical importance can find in their location at least one clear link to objectives of national significance. The region's economic potential and its prospective ability to contribute to the overall economic growth of the country is of course, another important asset. The greater the asset and the less expensive or complex its exploitation, the higher the region's prospects for mobilizing support. Another consideration is the electoral political potential of the region. Regions with larger populations tend to be more attractive to politicians looking for political rewards for their actions.

Finally, a most important factor is the extent of the region's physical, organizational and social integration. In regions where the population is split due to the spatial structure or to conflicts between economic, or ethnic groups, where there are no common interests between the different social entities; where there is no recognized regional leadership with general authority and other means of sustaining and motivating regional identity, such as regional symbols or institutions - the negotiating power of the region is likely to be poor. Social integration becomes even more essential when when the region lacks other 'potentialities,' since it may become its only future asset.

Having acquired the knowledge concerning the region's potentialities, a strategic choice must be made and the means for enhancing the bargaining position of the region have to be specified. One important function to be established is an information flow system. It is important that the local people are aware of the potentialities of their region in order to be able to translate them into real assets. Communication channels could be of much assistance and may need to be developed. Socialization processes could also be of the utmost significance, since they help people acquaint themselves with the other facets of the society within which they are live and operate *vis-á-vis* the external environment, and assist them in assuming new roles. Development resources should be allocated to promote regional integration, to enhance community activities designed to reduce internal gaps and to formulate common needs and aims. But more than anything else, organizations and leadership should be encouraged and regional development plans should include mechanisms for enhancing their ability to negotiate, as they will be the ones to conduct the dialogue with the centre on behalf of the region.

The emphasis on the negotiation capability of the regions as a key ingredient in the development strategy does not reduce the significance of other vital aspects. The capability to bargain and mobilize environmental resources by itself is not sufficient for development, but it is an essential factor in improving the changes of implementation and the continuity of development efforts.

NOTES

1. See, for example, Singer and Lamounier (1972) and Haddad (1981) on Brazil; Hewitt de Alcantana (1977) on Mexico.
2. For Peru see for instance, Cotler (1975), Smith (1976) Couriel (1978) and Hilhorst (1981).
3. Again in Peru, but also in Chile (Boisier, 1981; Garcia, 1973).
4. As is the case in Brazil (de Mattos, 1981).
5. See, for instance the cases of the Dominican Republic, Peru and Ecuador in I. Prion et al. (1981, 1982, 1983).
6. For a more extensive discussion see Weintraub and Margulies (1986).

REFERENCES

Barraclough, S. *Agrarian Structure in Latin America.* Lexington Books, 1971.
Boisier, S. "Chile: Continuity and Change - Variations of Centre-Down Strategies

Under Different Political Regimes." In *Development from Above or Below*, edited by W.R. Stohr and R.D. Fraser-Taylor. New York: John Wiley and Sons, 1981.

Cotler, J. "The New Mode of Political Denomination in Peru". In *Peru's Ambiguous Revolution, The Peruvian Experiment*, edited by A. Lowenthal, A. Princeton: Princeton University Press.

De Mattos, C.A. "Some Consequences of Growth and Spatial Concentrations in Latin American." In *Polarized Development and Regional Policies*, edited by A. Kuklinski, A. Tribute to Jaques Boudeville. The Hague: Mouton Publishers, 1981.

Feder, E. *Violencia Despojo del Campessino: el Latifundismo en America Latino.* Mexico: Segio Reitivmo Eli SA, 1972.

Garcia, A. *Reforma Agraria y Dominacion Social en America Latina.* Buenos Aires: Ediciones SIAP, 1973.

Haddad, P. R. "Brazil: Economic Efficiency and the Disintegration of Peripheral Regions," In *Development from Above or Below*, edited by W.R. Stohr and R.D. Fraser-Taylor. New York: John Wiley and Sons, 1981.

Hewitt de Alcantara, C. "Mexico: A Commentary on the Satisfaction of Basic Needs." In *Another Development Approach and Strategy*, edited by M. Nerfin. Uppsala: The Dag Hammerskjold Foundation, 1977.

Hilhorst, J.G.M. *Regional Planning in Peru: Top-Down or Bottom-Up.* The Hague: ISS Occasional Papers, 1980.

Hilhorst, J.G.M. "Peru: Regional Planning 1968-77; Frustrated Bottom-Up Aspirations in a Technocratic Military Setting" *Development from Above or Below*, edited by W.R. Stohr and R.D. Fraser-Taylor. John Wiley & Sons, 1981.

Kuitenbrowen, J. *The Functions of Social Mobilization in the Process Towards a New Society in Peru.* ISS Occasional Papers, The Hague.

Lefeber, L. "Normative and Institutional Problems in Regional Planning: Urban vs. Rural Development." In *Polarized Development and Regional Policies*, edited by A. Kuklinksi. Tribute to Jacques Boudeville, The Hague, New York: Mouton Publishers.

Matos-Mar, J. *La Reforma Agraria en el Peru.* Lima: Peru Problema, No. 13, IEP, 1980.

Prion, I., et al. *Proyectos de Planificacion de Desarrollo Rural Integrado de la Region Sur - Republica Dominicana* Rehovot: Fundacion David, Publicacion Sobre DRI CERUR, 1981.

Prion, I. et al. *Proyecto de Planificacion del Desarrollo Rural Integrado de la Region PACOSAN, Peru.* Rehovot: Fundacion David, Publicaciones Sobre DRI CERUR, 1982.

Prion, I. et al. *Proyecto de Planificacion del Desarrollo Rural Integrado de la Region Bolivar, Ecuador.* Rehovot: Fundacion David, Publicacion Sobre DRI, CERUR, 1983.

Rofman, A.B. *Dos Ensayos Sobre Planificacion Regional.* Beunos Aires: Centro de Estudios Urbanos y Regionales, 1982.

Schreider, H. *National Objectives and Project Appraisal in Developing Countries.* Paris: OECD, 1975.

Singer, P., and Lamounier. B. "Brazil: Growth Through Inequality." In Nerfin (ed.). *Op. cit. Another Development Approach and Strategy*, edited by M. Nerfin. Uppsala: The Dag Hammerskjold Foundation, 1977.

Weintraub, D., and Margulies, J. *Basic Social Diagnosis for IRRD Planning.* Aldershot: Gower Publishing Company, 1986.

DEVELOPMENT AGENCY/VILLAGER RELATIONS

Neal Sherman

The relations between development agencies and villagers form a special topic within the broader field of development administration, which constitutes a special sub-field within the general study of organization and administration. Administrative theory depicts a contrast between bureaucratic and professional styles in the organization of work, and this basic theoretical distinction lies at the heart of questions frequently raised in studies of field-level contacts between the rural population and representatives of development agencies. Empirically, is a field representative of the development agency best characterized as a bureaucrat, who functions within the framework of a detailed set of organizational regulations and is subject to close hierarchical supervision in order to guarantee faithful implementation of those regulations? Or is the field worker a professional, who solves problems as they arise through the application of advanced analytic skills to detailed firsthand knowledge of local conditions? Normatively, is the achievement of development goals best served by the design of the field worker's role along bureaucratic or professional lines?

These questions are relevant to the extent that it is believed that the performance of development agencies may be improved by adapting their organizational forms to the nature of the missions which confront them. Such a belief is commonly found among writers who see the special quality of development administration as deriving from the special nature of the development task, i.e. the conscious promotion of change. On the other hand, those who define development administration as administrative activity carried out within the particular political, social and economic environment of the Third World countries, tend to see the internal organization of work within the development agency as an issue of strictly limited significance.

In this paper, an attempt will be made to summarize central themes in the study of relations between development agencies and villagers through a review of the outlooks of the major schools in the development administration literature regarding the issue of bureaucratic *versus* professional execution of field activities. This review is followed by a presentation of new approaches to development administration, which provide new perspectives on the bureaucratic-professional contrast.

In keeping with the evolution of professional thought and actual policy, 'development agencies' will be taken as governmental agencies, until the idea of the non-governmental, voluntary organization as a development agency is introduced explicitly towards the conclusion of this paper.

BUREAUCRACY AND PROFESSIONALISM

In bureaucratic organizations, the bulk of staff know *what to do* by reference to a detailed corpus of written regulations which prescribe precise, organization-specific responses to the various situations that each worker is expected to encounter in the course of his duties. *Motivation to act in keeping with organizational needs* is provided by close hierarchical supervision, which makes use of the detailed regulations as criteria for the evaluation of workers' performance. By contrast, the professional worker is expected to discover independently *what to do* through the application of abstract analytic principles to the details of the particular situations with which he is confronted. For the most part, the analytic principles to be applied are not organization-specific, but rather are the joint property of members of the profession whatever their organizational affiliation. State of the art information concerning professional trends is diffused from academic centres of research and instruction by means of formal certificate-granting courses of study, special instructional activities, the activities of professional societies and the publication of books and journals. *Motivation to act in keeping with organizational needs* is to a certain extent a function of hierarchical evaluation of the professional's work, but it is also largely a function of internalized commitments: to the organization, to the profession, to political and social ideologies.

Obviously, even in a basically bureaucratic organization a certain stratum of top-level, rule-formulating functionaries will have to work as professionals. The question then arising is in which circumstances is it preferable that most workers in the organization be governed by detailed organizational regulations, and in which circumstances is it preferable that a broad cross-section of staff be expected to perform as professionals. The usual capsule response to this query states that bureaucratic organization is most appropriate when the organization's staff perform their roles in a simple, stable and therefore reliably predictable environment. On the other hand, when staff must contend with complex, changing circumstances which the organization cannot easily control or predict, it becomes necessary to allow them to adjust their activities in keeping with their own, *ad hoc* professional analyses of the situations facing them.(1)

THE 'DEVELOPMENTAL' CHARACTER OF DEVELOPMENT ADMINISTRATION

Two basic approaches may be found in the literature regarding the meaning attributed to 'development' in the term 'development administration'. The administrative ecology school sees the special character of development administration as deriving from the special characteristics of society in the developing nations. The most prominent exponent of this approach is Fred Riggs.(2) Riggs states as a general theoretical proposition that the quality of service provided by government administrative bodies to the public is a direct function of the pressures which elements within the public can bring to bear in order to reward or punish the administration, in keeping with its performance. The specific character of development administration in today's developing nations derives, then, from the fact that particular historical circumstances have brought them to a situation in which the administration is in fact overwhelmingly powerful *vis-à-vis* its environment. As a result, the administration is free to pursue an exploitative, self-serving, and indeed destructive course of action in its use of public authority and the material resources which stand at the disposal of the state.

To the extent that they treat the ongoing work of the state administrative apparatus, neo-Marxist, dependency theory oriented students of the Third World may also be classed with Riggs as administrative ecologists.(3) Their basic approach to understanding the functioning of administrative agencies is similar. However, unlike Riggs, who describes an environment in which there is no element whose power approaches that of the administration, the neo-Marxists see in international capital a powerful economic and political force to which the administration must accommodate its operations and whose interests the administration must strive to serve efficiently.

By contrast to the stress in administrative ecology analyses on the general balance of power between the administration and other forces within society, the administrative engineering school sees the special character of development administration as deriving from the particular challenges inherent in attempts to initiate and promote qualitative change in men's patterns of thought and behaviour.(4) Organization is a tool whose performance may be improved by adjusting its specific characteristics to the nature of the task it is called upon to perform. Organizational characteristics are taken as significant variables, whatever the overall characteristics of the society within which the organization functions. From this point of view Selznick's *TVA and the Grassroots* and *Implementation* by Pressman and Wildavsky are as much works on development administration as is Chambers' *Settlement Schemes in Tropical Africa*, despite the fact that the first two studies deal with twentieth-century United States.(5)

The stress in the administrative engineering approach on adapting the organization to deal with change leads in most cases to a tendency to recommend a loosening of bureaucratic controls, so as to allow greater leeway for professional discretion. This point will be further elaborated below with specific regard to the functioning of field staff who come into direct contact with the rural population. From the point of view of the administrative ecology school, which sees administrative functioning as a direct outcome of the overall balance of power between administration and its environment, the formal organization of work within government agencies seems a question of little significance. For ultimately, whatever the formal arrangements adopted, the substantive quality of performance will be determined by the ability, or inability, of interested groups to bring effective pressures to bear or to offer enticing rewards.

ADMINISTRATIVE ECOLOGY/ENGINEERING IN THE LOCAL-LEVEL CONTEXT

The two basic approaches to the nature of development administration, set forth above, provide two basic approaches to the analysis of villager/agency relations. The administrative ecology school conceives agency functioning at the local level as an outcome of the position of local staffers within, and in relation to, local society. The administrative engineering school interprets agency functioning as a function of organizational characteristics, i.e. the tasks imposed on local staff, the organization's style of operations and its effectiveness in imposing faithful implementation of organizational directives.

These contrasting outlooks are well illustrated in articles by Van Velzen and Leonard on staff-villager relations in rural Tanzania and Kenya, respectively.(6) Van Velzen's analysis depicts a situation very much in keeping with the basic hypotheses of administrative ecology. The local-level representatives of central government agencies constitute a distinct social grouping, whose members are clearly aware of their group and individual private interests, which are only partially related to the fulfillment of their formally assigned duties. Relations with the local community are based on the staff's desire to promote their own interests rather than on organizational needs, as defined by the letter and spirit of government policy.

The bulk of the local population have few resources with which to threaten or to reward staff, and so the staff ride roughshod over the average villagers. By contrast, the wealthy peasants can be of service to the staff in the *pro forma* fulfillment of certain organizationally determined tasks; in the general maintenance of orderly control over the local community; and in the provision of direct, personal and usually material benefits. The local level staff therefore form a coalition with the wealthy peasants in order to promote their own narrowly defined aims. The policies and operating characteristics of the organizations which local staff are supposed to represent and serve are of little relevance in explaining their actual behaviour and the resulting distribution of the benefits provided by the agencies to the villagers.

On the basis of his research in Kenya, Leonard reaches rather different conclusions, in line with administrative engineering's emphasis on the importance of organizational design as a factor affecting performance. In his attempt to explain a distribution of programme benefits, skewed, as in Van Velzen's Tanzanian case, in favour of local elite members, Leonard stresses the influence of a particular school of professional thought - the 'progressive farmer' approach to agricultural extension - as the major factor leading to the concentration of benefits upon those already better-off. In addition to the conceptual justification provided by a well developed body of professional thought, Leonard cites as a further contributing factor the greater willingness and ability of elite members to complain to supervisory staff regarding deficient service provided by field workers. Leonard also notes that through contact with progressive farmers, field workers are likely to achieve quicker, and easier introduction of improved farm practices, that is, quicker and easier achievement of the professional goals set for them by their organization. In short, the organization within which field staff function does matter: the reigning professional school of thought which shapes working method, the application of hierarchical discipline in response to client complaints, and organizational goals are relevant variables which must be taken into account to explain what happens in the field. The direct exchange of benefits between local staff and local elites in order to promote staff's private interests is a marginal, rather than a central, phenomenon.

BUREAUCRACY/PROFESSIONALISM IN THE LOCAL-LEVEL CONTEXT

It should be clear from the summary of Van Velzen's paper that an ecological approach to agency-villager relations tends to lead to the depiction of a deadlocked situation, in which the weight of power and interests prevent reform and improvement of administrative performance. Thus, just as Riggs' macro-social description of administration in developing countries leads to the conclusion that little can be achieved through organizational adjustments, so local level ecological studies lead to the conclusion that issues such as the opposition between bureaucratic and professional work styles are of little consequence.

Administrative engineering analyses, on the other hand, stress organizational design, and from their point of view the issue of bureaucracy versus professionalism seems relevant indeed. Considering this question in the context of agency-villager relations, what is in fact being asked is whether the chances are greater that centrally-formulated rules of operation will be appropriate guides to action, and will be corrected relatively quickly when evidence gathers that they are no longer appropriate; or, whether chances are greater that adequate solutions to operational difficulties will be devised by agency staff in the field, applying their professional skills to analysis of first-hand knowledge of local problems.

As indicated above, the emphasis in administrative engineering analyses on the adaptation of organization to the promotion of change may predispose adherents of this approach to recommend a basically professional organization of work. Consideration of certain aspects of the reality of day-to-day field work, however, suggests a somewhat more conservative, pro-bureaucratic set of conclusions. First of all, the demand to free field staff of bureaucratic burdens seems to assume that there exists in the field a well-spring of talent and creativity, waiting to burst forth once the stifling burden of bureaucratization is lifted. The oft-cited scarcity of skilled professional staff that plagues the developing countries would seem to suggest that this is not so, and that most field staff find it difficult, from a purely professional point of view, to deal with problems encountered in the course of their work. If this is so, the detailed codification of professional guidance in organizational routines would be required, rather than a grant of professional freedom, whose recipients are not fully competent to make use of such freedom. The challenge facing development administration would then be to achieve maximum exploitation of the capabilities of limited numbers of highly skilled professionals by incorporating their more advanced understanding in rules which can serve as a practical guide to action for less well qualified field workers.

Similarly, it may be recalled that the motivation to act in keeping with organizational goals is to be guaranteed in professionally-based systems by internalized value commitments. However, as just noted, the professional qualifications of the bulk of field staff are relatively low; moreover, sharp ethnic and class divisions plague many of the developing countries. Thus, it may well be doubted whether a sufficient proportion of field workers share some sufficiently strong commitment to a common body of organizational, professional, or socio-political ideological values, that may guarantee conscientious investment of effort in the field without the goad and guidance provided by active hierarchical supervision aimed at confirming the implementation of organizationally prescribed measures and the achievement of organizationally prescribed goals.

A further consideration which must be weighed when considering calls for debureaucratization relates to the fact that without clear guidelines in policy and in organizational regulations, the use to be made of official authority in a given field becomes the object of bargaining between agency staff and elements of the public directly affected by agency actions.(7) The question then arises whether efficiency and equity in the provision of services by development agencies are likely to be best served by hierarchical enforcement of centrally formulated regulations in the bureaucratic manner, or by a grant of broad discretionary authority to field level staff? Whose goals are likely to be more acceptable from the analyst's point of view: those of central policy makers or those of local elites, whose success in influencing the work of local staff is likely to be facilitated by broader grants of professional autonomy? Any attempt to formulate recommendations regarding the desirable organization of field work must be informed by an attempt to answer these questions on the basis of what is known in specific cases regarding the goals of policy makers and local elites and their relations with the state administrative apparatus.

A final point, which may be noted with regard to the question of bureaucracy versus professionalism in field work, is that though a number of authors write as if it is clear that development agencies in Third World countries suffer from overbureaucratization, the extent to which this generalization in fact holds true is an empirical question which must be re-examined with regard to the case of each agency and its operations. A number of studies, based on field research, reach opposite conclusions; that is, their findings suggest a situation of underbureaucratization, or perhaps 'premature professionalization'.(8) Political policy makers and senior administrative officials fear to take clear stands on controversial issues. Senior officials hesitate, as well, to risk their reputations by formulating their preferred solutions to complex professional problems as agency regulations, defining a clear, organizationally-prescribed working method. Thus, field staff may find themselves acting on many important, basic issues within a framework of vaguely defined general goals and a sparse sprinkling of operational instructions, rather than within the over-regulated situation generally presumed to exist.

FURTHER DEVELOPMENTS IN THE ANALYSIS OF DEVELOPMENT ADMINISTRATION

THE POLICY IMPLEMENTATION APPROACH

The basic presumption underlying those writings which are referred to here as reflecting a policy-implementation approach states that the particular characteristics of a given policy affect and activate the agency and its political and social environment in a particular fashion; that is, the interaction of organization and environment differs significantly in keeping with the differing character of the policies to be implemented. The major normative conclusion derived from this central insight is that the quality of agency-environment contacts likely to be engendered by the nature of policy must be taken into account in the formulation of policy. Furthermore, policy must include among its provisions guidelines regarding the adjustment of organizational structure and operational procedures to the specific characteristics of a given policy and the type of relations with the environment expected within the context of that policy. In particular, the balance between bureaucracy and professionalism in the organization of work should be determined with reference to the demands of particular policies.(9) Such an approach, then, integrates the emphasis of administrative ecology on the influence of the environment on organizational functioning with a more detailed application of administrative engineering's general emphasis on the need to adapt organization to the general goal of development policies, namely the promotion of significant change.

Cleaves' attempt to demonstrate the implications of "characteristics of policy affecting its implementation" for "policy design" may be cited as an example of the approach just outlined.(10) Cleaves sets forth the following list of criteria for the classification of policies according to the degree of difficulty attending their implementation:

Less Problematic	More Problematic
Simple technical features	Complex technical features
Marginal change from *status quo*	Comprehensive change from *status quo*
One-actor target	Multi-actor targets
One-goal objective	Multi-goal objectives
Clearly stated goals	Ambiguous or unclear goals
Short duration	Long duration

Concerned with attempts to implement policies intended to benefit the poor, Cleaves notes the typically limited administrative capabilities of government agencies in less developed countries, on the one hand, and the weakness of the poor as a clientele capable of organizing and acting so as to complement agency efforts to promote their welfare, on the other hand. He thus concludes that attempts to aid the poor must be embodied in policies which are less problematic in terms of his scheme. That is, when implementation difficulties are taken into account, policy making aimed at promoting the interests of the poor will focus on simple, discrete, short-term projects which yield immediate benefits. Given the emphasis on regional development in this collection of articles, it is particularly interesting to note that

Cleaves' approach clashes with the claims of those who present integrated area development methods as a means of serving the underprivileged. Integrated development policies would clearly fall into the 'more problematic' category on almost all criteria, and would therefore have to be classified as inappropriate to their professed goals of aiding the poor, once expected implementation difficulties are considered.

THE SOCIAL ENGINEERING APPROACH

The social engineering approach accepts the basic theoretical tenets of administrative ecology, but presents a somewhat more optimistic outlook regarding the possibility of improving administrative performance. Administrative ecology studies tend to present a stark depiction of overall social deadlock. Elites make use of their power so as to exploit and guarantee the continued subjugation of the disadvantaged. The perversion of the functioning of government agencies and of their relations with the middle and poor villagers constitute a major aspect of this repression. The analysis suggests, implicitly or explicitly, that little can be done, short of revolutionary change.

The social engineering approach recognizes the inefficiency and the stifling nature of government monopoly over development initiative in many field of activity in most less developed countries. However, social engineering, as opposed to administrative ecology, points out an opening for change: non-governmental, voluntary organizations (NGO's) are an element in the environment of administration which may be promoted as a means for the achievement of meaningful improvements in the performance of developmental activities, in general, and in the functioning of government agencies, in particular.(11) NGO's, first of all, carry out some development activities on their own, thus relieving an overburdened state apparatus of certain duties, according to one point of view, or breaking the state apparatus' monopoly, according to an alternative point of view. In addition, NGO's serve as an independent source of feedback regarding field-level operations of government agencies, and are capable of intervening and applying immediate pressures so as to affect those operations. Their presence and activity thus should serve as a factor leading to improvement in the performance of government agencies.

Finally, it is suggested that NGO's are more inclined to promote appropriate forms of local organization for development efforts, and to support such organization without stifling it through heavy-handed cooptation attempts. Through the encouragement of limited local organizations (LLO's), which are informal limited-purpose groupings based primarily on traditional forms of solidarity, NGO's help to promote among the village population, the ability to organize and act independently of governmental agencies. NGO's thus help to lay the foundations for a future situation in which an organized public will be able to exert effective pressures on the government to guarantee the honest, efficient and non-exploitative functioning of the state apparatus.

CONCLUSIONS

Those committed to promoting a progressive, egalitarian form of development in the Third World countries by means short of violent revolution, will have to approach the issue of development agency-villager relations with the insights of the more recently elaborated approaches to development administration in mind. Policy must be formulated with implementation difficulties explicitly taken into account. The prescription of organizational structure and operating methods, the determination of the mix of bureaucratic and professional elements appropriate to the achievement of specific policy goals, must be understood as an essential aspect of the policy maker's responsibility. Such organizational design adjustments must be based on a consideration of the interaction of government agencies with their environment, as engendered by the character of given policies. However, the environment need not be taken wholly as given. The overall range of development policies should include initiatives aimed at intensifying the activity of NGO's and LLO's as a complement and as a counterweight to the operations of governmental agencies.

NOTES

1. This section is based on Perrow (1972), Chapter 1.
2. Riggs (1964); Riggs (1963).
3. See, for example, Leys (1974), pp. 193-198, 249-250.
4. See, for example, Leonard (1977); Sherman (1981).
5. Selznick (1966); Pressman and Wildavsky (1973); Chambers (1969).
6. Van Velzen (1976); Leonard (1976).
7. This point is developed in the context of American politics in Lowi (1969).
8. Sherman (1981), pp. 160-161; also note the stress on the need to base field operations on formally defined routines in Kulp (1970) and Chambers (1974).
9. See Grindle (1980).
10. Cleaves (1980).
11. See Hyden (1983), Chapters 5, 6; Hunter (1981).

REFERENCES

Chambers, R. *Settlement Schemes in Tropical Africa*. London: Routledge & Kegan Paul, 1969.

--------. *Managing Rural Development: Ideas and Experience from East Africa*. Uppsala: The Scandinavian Institute of African Studies, 1974.

Cleaves, P.S. "Implementation Amidst Scarcity and Apathy: Political Power and Policy Design". In *Politics and Policy Implementation in the Third World*, edited by M.S. Grindle. Princeton: Princeton University Press, 1980.

Grindle, M.S. "Policy Content and Context in Implementation". In *Politics and Policy Implementation in the Third World*, edited by M.S. Grindle. Princeton: Princeton University Press, 1980.

Hunter, G. *A Hard Look at Directing Benefits to the Rural Poor and at "Participation"*. London: Overseas Development Institute, Discussion Paper 6, June 1981.

Hyden, G. *No Shortcuts to Progress*. Berkeley: University of California Press, 1983.

Kulp, E.M. *Rural Development Planning*. New York: Praeger Publishers, 1970.

Leonard, D.K. "The Social Structure of the Agricultural Extension Services in the Western Province of Kenya". In *Government and Rural Development in East Africa*, edited by L. Cliffe, J. S. Coleman, M. R. Doornbos. The Hague: Martinus Nijhoff, 1976.

--------. *Reaching the Peasant Farmer*. Chicago: University of Chicago Press, 1977.

Leys, C. *Underdevelopment in Kenya*. Berkeley: University of California Press, 1974.

Lowi, T.J. *The End of Liberalism*. New York: W.W. Norton, 1969.

Perrow, C. *Complex Organizations*. Glenview, Illinois: Scott, Foresman,1972.

Pressman, J.L. and Wildavsky, A.B. *Implementation*. Berkeley: University of California Press, 1973.

Riggs, F.W. "Bureaucrats and Political Development: A Paradoxical View". In *Bureaucracy and Political Development*,edited by J. La Palombara. Princeton: Princeton University Press, 1963.

--------. *Administration in Developing Countries*. Boston: Houghton Mifflin , 1964.

Selznick, P. *TVA and the Grass Roots*. New York: Harper and Row, 1966.

Sherman, N.P. "The Department of Cooperative Development: Administrative Aspects of Government Intervention". In *Cooperatives and Development*, by C. Young, N. P. Sherman, T. H. Rose. Madison: University of Wisconsin Press, 1981.

Van Velzen, H.U.E. "Staff, Kulaks and Peasants: A Study of a Political Field". In *Government and Rural Development in East Africa*, edited by L. Cliffe, J.S. Coleman, M.R. Doornbos. The Hague: Martinus Nijhoff, 1976.

REGIONAL COOPERATION AND SPATIAL RELATIONS IN THE RURAL SECTOR

Rachel Wilkansky

INTRODUCTION

One characteristic which differentiates between the rural and the urban sectors is the need for cooperation which pervades the rural sector. The rural sector, trying to counter natural hazards as well as marketing difficulties, has turned to cooperation as a means of pooling resources and providing mutual help. The basic advantage of cooperation in all its forms is therefore an economic one: it strives to improve both production and welfare through the use of scale economies and through increased efficiency in the use of agricultural means of production. Cooperation also has an important ideological basis: it strives to foster equity in the rural sector by creating an equal base for all partners, but in fact this ideology is often expressed in economic terms, as for instance in the setting of production quota in agricultural planning.

Numerous agricultural cooperatives exist in various countries, but other organizational forms of cooperation can be found as well. All the organizations of rural cooperation function within a formal organizational framework which affects their effectiveness and their relationships with the surrounding environment. The supporting role of this organizational framework is essential to ensure a continuing process of rural development. At the same time, the organizational framework itself is affected by the changing patterns of development: it evolves and takes on different forms at different levels of development. The fostering of an optimum organizational framework, adaptable to specific stages of development, is therefore a crucial question in the formulation of rural development policies.

The purpose of this paper is therefore twofold: to describe the organizational framework of cooperation within the rural sector and the changes occurring in this framework in the process of development or changes which might be desirable; and to show some of the spatial implications of rural cooperation and organization.

While being of a general nature, the following presentation draws heavily on Israel's experience which is a good example for several reasons:

1. Israel has been through rapid change during the last decades and has reached a relatively high level of development: much can therefore be learned from the evolution of rural organization at the different stages of development.
2. The great diversity of regions in Israel allows for the identification of general patterns common to all, while special cases can also be studied.
3. An almost complete separation between the urban and the rural sectors has accompanied the development of Israel. Thus processes of change occurring within the rural sector alone, as well as advantages and disadvantages of this separation, can be studied.

Indeed, cooperation at the local level has been the accepted basis for most rural settlement in Israel. Cooperation was the natural outgrowth of a pervading social solidarity and a collective will to work for development. Thus most rural settlements are cooperatives (moshavim) or even collectives (kibbutzim). However, in Israel as in other countries cooperation at the local level has proven insufficient in spite of its effectiveness; the need for a wider scale of cooperation led to cooperation at the regional level.

COOPERATION AT THE REGIONAL LEVEL

Various regions differ by their specific physical, social and economic characteristics, and each region evolves its own pattern of cooperation. Yet a general pattern of evolution can be identified. The first goals of cooperation at the regional level are usually 'basic services', mainly municipal services such as drainage, water supply, sewage disposal, road construction or malaria control, and basic services to agriculture such as the supply of agricultural inputs, credit and marketing services. Some social services, such as education, are also often the subject of early cooperation. Individual settlements are sometimes reluctant to give up their independence in these matters, but they have to accept the fact that regional cooperation implies a trade-off between the gains which can be achieved and the loss of local autonomy.

The processing of agricultural products in agro-industrial enterprises located within the region develops at a later stage of regional cooperation, and the latest form of regional cooperation in Israel includes the creation of regional colleges which provide higher-level education for the rural population.

Thus cooperation in the rural sector evolves not only from a local to a regional level, but also from basic services to the processing of agricultural products and to a more sophisticated type of services.

THE ORGANIZATIONAL FRAMEWORK OF COOPERATION IN ISRAEL

Each one of the different types of services has become organized in a pattern suited to its needs. A whole system of organizations has thus developed, mostly in a parallel manner, with little formal overlapping, at different scales of action (national or regional) and with different organizational set-ups as follows:

1. Municipal services are provided by the local government which is typical of rural areas in Israel i.e. the Regional Councils, which are elected by the inhabitants of the region but are highly dependent on the national government for their financial resources.

2. These Regional Councils are also responsible for the provision of most social services in the rural settlements.

3. Extension services are provided by the Ministry of Agriculture through its regional offices.

4. For the supply of agricultural inputs and needed credit, the settlements have organized into purchasing organizations at a regional scale, but not necessarily defined on a territorial basis.

5. Marketing services have been the responsibility of a national marketing organization which is a secure and stable outlet for agricultural produce and which has set-up a sophisticated system for the distribution of produce all over the country.

6. Finally, for the processing of agricultural products the settlements have set up regional organizations, sometimes related to - or even part of - the older purchasing organizations, and these have been gaining a central position in the development of the region.

In addition to all these organizations, each settlement belongs to one of the National Settlement Movements which acts as its representative in all matters. These movements are comprehensive organizations; their purpose is to promote the development of individual settlements and to help them solve their problems as they arise, whether these are of an economic, social or other nature.

Some friction has become apparent between the national organizations (such as the Settlement Movements) and the regional organizations as to their respective role in relation to the individual settlements, and a rough division of functions has been agreed upon: The National Settlement Movements are responsible for ideological, political and social issues, while regional organizations take care of functional and economic problems, such as purchasing supplies, ensuring credit or providing the needed infrastructure. The National Purchasing Organizations which are directly subordinated to the Settlement Movements, limit their role to the purchasing of consumer goods and heavy agricultural equipment, while the Regional Purchasing Organizations provide inputs and credit.

All these organizations, whether national or regional, are integrated within a roof organization, the Agricultural Centre of the Labour Union, which serves as the focus of all organizations dealing with the rural sector. In addition to the organizations already mentioned above, a whole network of national organizations dealing with problems and needs of the rural settlements, is affiliated to the Agricultural Centre. These organizations handle a great variety of subjects, such as legal problems, mutual insurance, accounting or agricultural education and research. They also include professional Growers' Associations and even the Association of Regional Councils.

The Agricultural Centre is therefore the main forum for coordination between all these bodies. It also is the center of negotiations with the national government on policies concerning agriculture and settlement. The Agricultural Centre, together with the affiliated National Settlement Movements, has been the main force in promoting and ensuring a lasting national commitment to goals of rural development and social equity.

The relationships between all these organizations within the Agricultural Centre are characterized by a considerable degree of connectedness, which goes much beyond their formal framework. In each organization, the central council is formally elected at regular intervals. However there is also a periodical reshuffling of key officials within the Agricultural Centre and its affiliated organizations. This reshuffling takes place mainly on the basis of personal acquaintance and appreciation. Some officials may perform two roles simultaneously; they may, for instance, be elected to the central council of a regional purchasing organization and, at the same time, be appointed to a key post within a national organization. This connectedness ensures a stable basis of agreement and coordination between the different organizations, as well as a relatively high level of participation of local leadership in the national scene. The influence of the Agricultural Centre has become so dominant that it has even gained formal recognition and influence in other national agencies which are created by law and fulfill planning and advisory functions in the elaboration of agricultural policies. Such agencies include for instance the Production and Marketing Boards for the various branches of agricultural production, or the General Agricultural Council that deals with national agricultural policy. In these agencies we can find both appointed government officials and a very high proportion of representatives of the rural population, often more than half. These representatives are appointed by agreement with and upon the advice of the Agricultural Centre, and are usually chosen from among the key officials of the Agricultural Centre itself. Thus the highly integrative character of the whole system is reinforced; so is also the influence of the rural organizations, and through them the influence of the rural population on the national agricultural and settlement development policies.

In spite of the oversized bureaucracy created by the great number of different organizations involved, this combination of organizations at the national and regional levels has created a highly articulated and stable system which effectively combines local and regional solidarity with the enlarged scale of national organization. The numerous linkages existing within this system, horizontally and vertically, ensure a great measure of concordance between national goals and planning and the local village units, in great part through the intermediate regional level.

SOME PRINCIPLES OF SUCCESSFUL ORGANIZATION FOR RURAL DEVELOPMENT

The Israeli experience which has been succinctly described above concurs with the experience in developing countries (Uphoff and Esman, 1974 and 1982), and shows that a multi-level articulate system of rural organizations is needed to ensure a stable and orderly development of the rural sector. However, the process of building such an organizational system is no less important than its end result. It has been found, in Israel and elsewhere (Cernea, 1974) that there is a gradual process of integration of the individual settlement with its neighbours and then into the wider regional cooperative framework. Moreover, the increasing scale of co-operation is accompanied by an increasing complexity and multiplicity of regional cooperative activities. Cooperation normally starts between neighbouring villages: accounting and management services are jointly hired and cultural facilities are jointly used. Cooperation then widens into the realm of municipal services. Gradually, the activities which are undertaken jointly multiply, involve more settlements and become more complex, until they include, as described earlier, sophisticated processing industries or institutions of higher education.

This gradual evolution into a supra-local and then into a regional framework has some practical advantages. At the first stages of development, the financial resources needed can be minimized by inter-village cooperation; but the gradual enlargement of scale also contributes to a gradual restructuring of the region, following the break up of local traditional groupings. The disruptive effect of change inside the villages can be minimized by the growth of organizations providing suitable adaptive mechanisms. For example, the modernization of agriculture leads to specialization, and this in turn creates a great degree of differentiation between farmers within the same settlement. Groups of farmers are thus created with differing economic interests, and the small local cooperative is unable to handle efficiently the needs of all the groups. One solution might be to force a uniform pattern of agricultural production on all the farms in a village, so that the local cooperative can again provide for the identical needs of all. A more flexible solution may be provided by the gradual creation of intervillage associations of farmers with similar interests; such a structure may cause a profound change in the character of local cooperatives, which will hand over some of their functions to new supra-local or regional organizations.

The dynamic character of the organizational framework is therefore very important. Organizations must be flexible and able to adapt themselves easily to changes; they must be able to counteract the disruptive influences of modernization and of changes in the scale of agricultural operations.

Another characteristic of a successful organizational framework for rural development relates to the linkages of regional organizations within the wider social system. There is, no doubt, a need for coordination between the different regional organizations, and this can be achieved only at the national level: weak coordination and the lack of enforcement of an agreed-upon common policy have resulted, in Israel, in duplication of regional enterprises, of which some are now working at below-efficiency levels.

In addition to regional coordination, there is also a need for implementation of national policies down to the local level, and regional organizations are an important channel for the execution of national plans and programs. As already mentioned, the budgets of Regional Councils in Israel are in great part allocated by the national government, and this allows for national control over regional and local activities for which the Regional Councils are responsible. On the other hand, when central directives strongly dominate the regional and local scene, there is a gradual weakening of motivation and of initiative in the rural population, and the pace of development slows down. In order to be effective, the formation of rural organizations must be compatible with local needs. Only then can it be reinforced by the common interests and shared identity of farmers at the local level. Furthermore, rural organizations should be based on local and regional initiative, so that they have the whole-hearted support of the population.

Effective organization, however, requires considerable resources and leadership; and - at least in the beginning - help from the national level is essential. It is unlikely that rural organizations can be effective without strong central support and without some outside control counteracting vested interests of local minorities. Even Israel's kibbutzim, with their strong tradition of self-help and initiative, have always had the support, financial or other, of their Settlement Movement and through it, of the national government. They have thus been able to achieve a relatively high level of development, much beyond their basic agricultural potential.

It therefore seems that in building the organizational system of the rural sector, neither the top-down nor the bottom-up approach alone can provide the solution, and a combination of the two approaches is needed. At the early stages of development help from above must be provided to the local and regional organizations; then an articulate organizational system at the local and regional levels must be established gradually, and strengthened with both horizontal and upwards channels of communication.

REGIONAL INTEGRATION

The system of rural organizations in Israel is relatively fragmented. Although there is a central coordinating and controlling agency - the Agricultural Centre, there is also a multiplicity of organizations, each one with its own purpose, its specific set-up and scale of action. The benefits of this specialization of rural organizations, and the inefficiency and poor-coordination of services due to the excessive proliferation of specialized organizations, have been noted in the relevant literature.

Some attempts at regional horizontal integration have been made in various countries. In one of the regions, for instance, in Israel the poultry branch has been integrated from the production of eggs to the processing of poultry-meat, taking advantage of all the possible backward and forward linkages, within the same region. The development of one section of this branch is dependent on and coordinated with the development of the others, and a continuous balance is achieved between all the sections of the branch which is, so to speak, self-contained within the region.

Beyond this, few comprehensive regional organizations seem to exist. Moreover, in Israel there is practically no territorial overlapping between the different organizations in one region. This lack of spatial overlapping is due to the differential tendency of the types of settlement to participate in a regional organization. This tendency depends, naturally, on the specific needs of the settlement, but it is also strongly linked to the value system prevalent in the settlement. In the kibbutz, for instance, there is a strong in-group emphasis and a negative orientation to other socio-economic systems. Therefore, cooperation with distant kibbutzim, which have the same social outlook and the same value system, is more legitimate and often preferred to cooperation with neighbouring but different communities. Exceptions can be found, in which the cooperative framework is defined pragmatically with no relation to the value system of the settlement, but on the whole, the differentiation between settlement types is a decisive factor in shaping the organizational framework. Spatial factors are not being considered and without a territorial basis for organization no feeling of regional identity can be created.

One outstanding example can be found in the south of Israel, in a region settled by kibbutzim only. The management of the regional enterprises there overlaps with the territory of the Regional Council, creating a situation in which the economic region is identical to the physical and administrative regions. The settlements themselves are homogeneous in structure, in interests and in development level, and the numerous common interests reinforce the regional solidarity between settlements. An intensive network of intervillage organizational ties and links and of cooperation at the regional level is emerging, creating a strong sense of regional integration and identity.

By contrast, other regions which have a heterogeneous settlement pattern, organizations are formed not on a territorial basis but according to economic or other interests. No spatial overlapping and no regional territorial identity exist.

It can then be concluded that an overlapping spatial framework of the various rural organizations contributes significantly to the formation of a territorially-based and integrated regional identity.

THE SPATIAL FOCUS OF REGIONAL COOPERATION

The functional and organizational relationships within the rural sector are expressed physically in the form of regional plants, regional schools and other regional facilities. The location of these regional facilities, i.e. the spatial arrangement of social and economic activities in the region, influences the access of rural settlements to regional services and the pattern of production and exchange in the region (Rondinelli and Ruddle, 1978).

In general the location of regional facilities is closely related to the system of urban centers which provide services to the region, and thus regional towns are reinforced and serve as foci of regional identity. In Israel, however, the rural and urban sectors are separated, and the rural sector has developed its own physical set-up unconnected with the urban environment. Thus regional facilities are located in 'rural centers' of which there are two types:

1. *Service centers*, which include regional services, such as schools, sport and cultural facilities, dispensaries, etc. The people providing the services are living in these centers, thus bringing a population of professionals into the rural sector.

2. The so-called "silent" centers, which include regional economic enterprises of grading, sorting, packing and processing of agricultural products, and some social services. In this case, workers in the regional enterprises do not live in the rural center, but live either in one of the rural communities or in an urban center located in the vicinity.

The location of rural centers is subordinated to considerations of the rural sector only, e.g. 'silent' centers are often located near an urban center which provides them with the needed labour force. The density and dispersion of rural centers depend on the density of rural settlements and on the needs of the rural population, but no integration within the general settlement system has been sought. In fact, though these rural centers constitute the tangible expression of the separation between the urban and the rural sectors, they are the first link between the two: workers from urban centers come to work there and thus a daily link is created with the urban sector. Moreover, the centers may assume an urban character, as a result of the functions they fulfill and the character of their professional and heterogeneous population.

In the past, the accepted policy has been to prevent these rural centers from growing and to keep them at a stationary level to avoid a competition with parallel urban settlements and services. In time, however, the rural population has grown but agricultural means of production have remained limited; a solution is therefore required within the region if outmigration is to be avoided. Since the separation between the rural and the urban sectors is perpetuated, consideration has been given to the enlargement of some rural centers so that they can absorb within the rural environment the sons and daughters who cannot remain on the farm and are employed in neighboring urban centers. Indeed, it seems that the growth and physical development of such rural centers is unavoidable. It is well-known that physical investments are practically irreversible and have long-range spatial implications, and rural centers will soon be competing with the neighboring towns: they assume some of the traditional functions of the town and they absorb some of the population that would naturally flow into the towns.

The separation between the rural and the urban sectors thus leads to a proliferation of small, rural, urbanizing centers, both rural centers and small towns. For the rural population, this proliferation provides an improved access to social services and to the economic infrastructure needed for the development of agriculture. However, the parallel and unrelated organizations of the rural and the urban systems, which are spatially interwoven within the same region, result in an inefficient use of similar services.

This situation brings to the fore some questions pertaining to the stages of development of the rural sector: how far can and should the rural sector internalize its own development potential without the help of intensive exchanges and relationships with the surrounding environment? What is the breaking point, or the threshold, beyond which relationships with the towns must be intensified, or else the rural sector itself must become urbanized? Answers to these questions are dependent on the prevailing value system; for instance, the kibbutzim in Israel have preferred to urbanize to a very high degree while isolating themselves from the surrounding settlement system. In general, however, it can be concluded that urban-rural relationships are bound to intensify with a more advanced level of development in the rural part of the region. Thus it seems desirable to ensure, from the start a simultaneous and balanced development of both towns and rural settlements within a common organizational framework by creating positive linkages between the two sectors, fostering collaboration in numerous aspects of development.

CONCLUSIONS

Obviously, in respect to organization for rural cooperation and development, the decisive importance of specific local traditions and value systems cannot be overemphasized. Indeed the case of Israel is a special one, but as Israel has already passed through different stages of the development process and has achieved a relatively high level of development, its example can be instructive for developing countries. Desirable as well as undesirable results of different organizational frameworks in the rural sector can be studied, and some guidelines can be provided as to the more suitable strategies of organizational development which will allow for a flexible adaptation to changing development levels.

REFERENCES

Bar-On, D. and Niv, A. "The Regional Development of the Kibbutz in the 80's: Alternatives to the Deterministic Approach." *Journal of Applied Behavioural Science* 19 (1983): 319-335.

Cernea, M. "Organizational Build-Up and Reintegrative Regional Development in Planned Agriculture." *Sociologia Ruralis* 14 (1974): 30-44.

Esman, M.J. and Uphoff, N.T. *Local Organization and Rural Development: The State of the Art*, Ithaca: Center for International Studies, Cornell University, 1982.

Gonen, A. and Weintraub, D. "Towards a Sociological Analysis of Regional Development." *Sociologia Ruralis* 14 (1974): 15-29.

Gonen, A. and Weintraub, D. "Community Characteristics and Differential Regional Participation." *Sociologia Ruralis* 16 (1976): 7-22.

Kellerman, A. "Spatial Aspects of the Interrural Centers of Israel." *Journal of Rural Cooperation* 4 (1976): 51-71.

Kowalak, T. "Issues and Problems of Regional Cooperative Integration in Polish Agriculture." *Journal of Rural Cooperation* 4 (1976): 3-15.

Rondinelli, D.A. and Ruddle, K. *Urbanization and Rural Development: A Spatial Policy for Equitable Growth* . New York: Praeger, 1978.

Uphoff, N.T., and Esman, M.J. *Local Organization for Rural Development: Analysis of Asian Experience*. Ithaca: Center for International Studies, Cornell University, 1974.

Weitz, R. *Regional Cooperation in Israel*. Publications on Problems of Regional Development, No. 1. Rehovot: Settlement Study Centre, 1964.

Young, C., Sherman, N.P. and Rose, T.H. *Cooperatives and Development - Agricultural Politics in Ghana and Uganda* . Madison: University of Wisconsin Press, 1981.

ABOUT THE AUTHORS

RAPHAEL BAR-EL is an economist, involved in research and teaching at the Settlement Study Centre, Rehovot (Israel), and at Ben-Gurion University, Beer Sheva (Israel). He specializes in rural economic development, rural industrialization and industrial technology. Theoretical and empirical analyses in these fields have been published in articles and books. Bar-El teaches economic development, industrial planning and research methodology at Ben-Gurion University in Israel, and at Cornell University in Ithaca, New York, and conducts courses on integrated rural development and on rural industrial planning to students from developing countries at training institutes in Israel and in Latin American countries.

AVROM BENDAVID-VAL is a regional economist on the staff of the Settlement and Resource System Cooperative Agreement, specializing in methodologies of regional analysis, processes of regional development planning and rural-urban dynamics. He has published widely, and has extensive experience as analyst, planner and trainer in both industrialized and non-industrialized countries.

GERALD J. KARASKA is Professor of Geography at Clark University, specializing in regional analysis and development planning. He has published extensively in his field and is Editor of Economic Geography. Dr. Karaska has research experience in Western, East European and developing countries. He is Director of the Settlement and Resource Systems Cooperative Agreement for Clark University.

JULIA MARGULIES is a sociologist and Head of the Research Division at the Settlement Study Centre, Rehovot (Israel), where she also teaches sociology of regional development in the postgraduate international courses on integrated rural development. Margulies specializes in the rural community and rural organization and has published several books and articles in her subject. She is a regular participant in SSC's planning teams and has been on projects conducted in Peru, the Dominican Republic, Ecuador and Colombia.

MICHAEL L. McNULTY is a Professor of Geography and Director of the Center for International and Comparative Studies at the University of Iowa. He has published numerous articles in scholarly journals and contributed to books dealing with problems of urban and regional development in the Third World. He has extensive research experience in Asia and Africa, is a member of the Board of Directors of the African Studies Association, and serves on the editorial board of several international journals.

MICHAEL PAINTER is an anthropologist with the Institute for Development Anthropology. He has conducted research on agricultural production and marketing in several regions of the Andes - most extensively in southern Peru - and on settlement and regional development in the eastern lowlands of Bolivia. He is the author of articles in the Journal of Peasant Studies, Latin American Research Review, Studies in Comparative Internal Development and other journals, and has contributed to a number of edited works on international development.

ISRAEL PRION is a Senior Planner and Researcher at the Settlement Study Centre in Rehovot (Israel), specializing in the methodology of regional planning of the economic sectors and specifically in the planning of the services sector and of spatial organization. He headed interdisciplinary teams for regional development planning in Latin America,.Africa and South-East Asia in the years 1974-1985 (Brazil, Chile, Bolivia, Ecuador, Peru, Dominican Republic, Costa Rica, Thailand, Ghana, Malawi), and serves as a lecturer in the postgraduate courses for integrated rural development at the Settlement Study Centre.

DENNIS A. RONDINELLI is a Senior Policy Analyst in the Office of International Programs at the Research Triangle Institute, Research Triangle Park, North Carolina. He has edited or authored nine books on international development policy, development management and urban and regional development in the Third World, and has published extensively on these topics in scholarly and professional journals. Rondinelli serves as a consultant to USAID, the World Bank and various United Nations agencies.

GERARD RUSHTON is Professor of Geography and Research Associate in the Center for Health Services Research, University of Iowa. He has conducted field studies in India and has reviewed pilot projects to improve health services in the Philippines and in Bolivia. He has written extensively on the problems of improving geographical accessibility to services in developing countries.

DAFNA SCHWARTZ is a researcher in economics at the Settlement Study Centre, Rehovot (Israel), specializing in industrial decentralization, government policy and incentives for industrial development in peripheral regions, and the role of secondary cities in rural development. Her publications analyse various theoretical aspects of government intervention and present case-studies in specific secondary towns.

NEAL SHERMAN is a political scientist, Senior Researcher at the Settlement Study Centre, Rehovot (Israel), and a lecturer in the SSC regional planning course, in the Department of Political Science at Tel Aviv University, and at the Ruppin Institute. His research projects focus on the organizational and social problems of moshav-type settlements. Sherman is co-author of Cooperatives and Development: Agricultural Politics in Ghana and Uganda, and has also published a number of articles on the Israeli rural sector and on research carried out at the SSC.

RACHEL WILKANSKY is a city and regional planner, Senior Researcher at the Settlement Study Centre, Rehovot (Israel). Her main interests include urban and regional development policy, town planning, urban-rural relationships and spatial and organizational aspects of development. She has been involved in various urban and regional planning projects in Israel and has published a number of articles and reports on planning and development problems in Israel. She has taught at the Technion (Israel Institute of Technology), and is currently teaching at the Centre for Urban and Regional Studies at Tel Aviv University.

INDEX

E

F

G

H

I

K

L

M

S

T

U

V

W

3